SUNN

A Mother's Intimate Journey Through
the Death of Her 19-year-old Daughter

Sariah Ellsmore

Library of Congress Cataloging-in-Publication Data

Ellsmore, Sariah.

ISBN: 978-1-944066-22-2

Printed in the United States of America

1 2 3 4 5 6 7 8 9 10

Contents

Preface   5

Foreword   9

Introduction   13

Chapter 1: Sunn   15

Chapter 2: January   39

Chapter 3: February   50

Chapter 4: March   56

Chapter 5: April   68

Chapter 6: May   72

Chapter 7: June   79

Chapter 8: July   84

Chapter 9: August   90

Chapter 10: September   93

Chapter 11: October   103

Chapter 12: November   108

Author's Note   120

Preface

I met Sariah Ellsmore seven years ago, when we started playing roller derby. Her easy laughter and adventurous spirit immediately endeared her to me and our entire team. Over the years, I have seen her take on challenges and confront any problem with a positive, all-or-nothing approach and winning smile. Sariah is not a whiner, and she has encouraged me to be the best version of myself—holding me and others to the same high standards she holds herself. She and her children immediately became like family. I am not the only one who feels this way and has welcomed the Ellsmores into their hearts.

I knew her daughter, Juliana, more than the other kids, as I was in an alternative classroom with her and privy to some of the things that were happening in her life. She was animated and extravagant, dramatic and creative. Above all else and regardless of any of the choices she made, she had a heart of gold. Like her mother, she was the first one to offer a positive word to boost up a friend. When she was killed in a tragic auto-mobile accident right before Christmas, our entire small mountain town was stunned and in mourning.

When my family and I entered the Ellsmore home several days later for Juliana's party, the beauty was overwhelming. Hanging snowflakes, pictures of Juliana, hearts, princess doo-dads and glitter filled the entire living room. This was a party to celebrate Juliana's life and see her off to the other world. Sariah greeted us with a tiara upon her head and dressed in white. Darren had painted his nails purple for his little girl. The room was filled with stories and laughter. Yes, there were tears, but there were more smiles because of the exuberant way in which Juliana lived. People of all ages came together, drank (and even smoked) together to remember this beautiful young woman who could belt out a song like there was no tomorrow. So many of Juliana's friends were there, and I could tell that they felt like they were part of the Ellsmore family too. I watched Sariah—the great momma—hold and comfort the children who mourned their lost friend. She gave each and every person there a piece of her, although I couldn't imagine how she had anything left after losing her daughter. Still, she gave and loved and held everyone in her wide arms.

That moment—as I watched her care for everyone else and wondered who was taking care of her—I saw the depth of Sariah's greatness. I felt humble. In the months that followed, I continued to see a woman who inspired others to live and love, even from within her own deep loss and mourning. I've always thought that it is important to talk about those who've crossed over and to acknowledge the power of death—particularly as it impacts the breadth of our ability to live—rather than shy away from the difficult conversations. Sariah and I have shared many of those conversations over the past year. Conversations about the true nature of our souls and the ways in which life carries on even after we shed our physical bodies. Conversations about how love transcends the veil between the worlds. After each conversation, I am left feeling uplifted and hopeful, not sad and fearful. Sariah's words and actions are an example of how precious life is and how important it is to bravely live it. Every single time, I am inspired and feel a great sense of love. Sariah has turned what I would think of as the worst possible thing into a way to bring more meaning and joy into life and to connect with others and the spirit that exists beyond us all. Every single day, she inspires me.

When Sariah told me about her book, I was excited that the world could experience the grace and hope that she has brought into my life. I know that others will feel comforted within her words and curious within her ponderings. I hope that anyone who has experienced the loss of a child will find all of the beautiful reasons there are to keep living. Sariah's zest for life and tenacious ability to see the good in all shines through the experiences that she shares. And her daughter, Juliana, lives on from within these pages. I know that she has helped to

Foreword

> Life is either a daring adventure or nothing.
>
> Helen Keller

There are only two ways to look at life: as though nothing is a miracle or as though everything is a miracle.

Albert Einstein

Memorial obituary

I was asked to write an obituary for my daughter when she passed away, but I couldn't bring myself to do it. It has taken almost a full year of grieving and processing the death to be able to finally allow these words to leave me.

December 18, 2017

Juliana Sunn Ellsmore, age 19, passed away from a car accident on Wolf Creek Pass, 28 miles from her home in Pagosa

Springs, Colorado. She was driving from her school in Denver, Colorado, to visit with her family for Christmas vacation. It is believed she fell asleep at the wheel and drove her car off the steep cliff edge of Highway 160. The cause of death was blunt force trauma, and she was determined to have died instantly.

She is survived by her parents, Darren and Sariah Ellsmore, and her siblings, Kalei, Hunter, Kirra and Malaya Ellsmore.

Juliana was a wonderful person, loved by all those who had the privilege of knowing her. She was a kind-hearted, beautiful soul who shared encouragement and support to the many friends she adored.

She loved many things, from children to animals, travel, music and the arts.

Her family has set up a scholarship in her honor, allowing for young people in the Pagosa area to receive musical training.

This day will be forever etched into the hearts of the family and friends of this young woman, remembering her beauty and love, her spunky attitude and her gracious presence. She will be dearly missed.

I am an average, middle-aged, American woman, mother of four children, married for 23 years. I'm a small business owner and a helicopter pilot. I fill my days with as much fun and love I can manage, and I am always looking for a good adventure. My views of life are pretty simple, as I like to stay neutral and open to new ideas. I have a curious nature and love to question the meaning and purpose of life. I can say, for the most part, my life has been a happy existence filled with love, family, travel and learning.

This past year has been a tornado of an experience. My entire life has shifted from carefree, easy living to one of torment, grief, loss, depression, extreme inquiry and solitude. I have had to dig deeper than I ever knew possible to meet a part of myself I didn't know existed. I learned how to surrender to life's torturous events and to feel my way to a new and profound place of wonder.

What I am left with is an entirely new perspective and a beautiful message. It is one of love and connection from the world beyond.

In my darkest hour of excruciating pain, I learned there is so much more to our existence than what we see and feel in real time.

Our loved ones never really leave us, and they want us to live the most meaningful, glorious lives possible. They experience through us and with us in every moment. We are never alone. I believe this is why they come through—to help us come to grips with our loss and emotion knowing they are still here.

I'm writing this story simply because I have to. This need is so strong in me, I am risking my outward appearance, criticism and skepticism to bring it to you. I simply feel deeply in my heart that if you are reading this story, then there is a reason for it. I hope to be able to convey my message in a way that will bring greater awareness and purpose to your life.

Our experiences can expand us if we allow them.

The words you are about to read are the tiny little pieces of my shattered heart mending their way back to wholeness.

I know at some point, we all go through heartbreak and loss and grief and sadness. Death is part of life.

I just want you to know you don't have to do it alone. You are not alone. Please know, I am here for you. As Juliana wrote in the lyrics of her song SMILE, "life is worth it and you are so precious to me."

With all the love in my heart I give you,

~SUNN

Introduction

Believe it or not, I have always been fascinated with death. For as long as I can remember, I have been curious with the existence of an afterlife and how to connect with it.

As a young woman, I used to volunteer with hospice and would sit with the dying. I would hold their hands and rub lotion on their feet. I would brush their hair and listen to the stories of these people ready to leave our world. They would talk about all the people they loved and the moments they were proud of in their lives. They would also talk to unseen visitors who were there ready to escort them to the other side.

I believed deeply there is something waiting for us all, and when the time is right, we will simply move on to a better place.

One of the elderly gentlemen came to me in a dream the night he passed; he thanked me for my visits and said goodbye.

When my daughter made her transition, my fascination was no longer just a curiosity but now a desperate need for answers. I had to know. I had to communicate.

If she chose me to be her mother, then she must have known prior to her earthly existence that I was going to travel this journey in search of an explanation. Her life was going to mean something and her death was going to be a doorway for all of us to get information and comfort.

I asked for assistance daily. I wrote in my journals religiously. Writing became my solace and my connection.

My daughter found a way to inspire my mind with beautiful messages from beyond, sharing her love and wisdom with me, and now with you.

I have opened my journals and blog posts to you as an intimate expression of my perspective as a mother in pain and now joy.

Note, communication from spirit is italicized.

~Enjoy~

Chapter 1

Sunn

My dear sweet Juliana, this book is for you. It is really for all of us who knew you and loved you. We are all just trying to get our bearings after your sudden and tragic escape from this world.

Dear daughter, where do I start? I love you so much my heart feels like a giant hole has been shot right through it. This hole is so big, nothing can fill it. The edges are cauterized, and if you stand in front of me, you can see right through my body and soul to the other side. Somehow, I'm still miraculously walking around. I'm breathing, I'm eating, I'm feeling and even as crazy as it sounds, I'm laughing. This humongous crater has caused my world to shift, and it has opened me up to a magnificent world beyond.

I know without a doubt you are still here. I know the communication I feel is real and the sweet symbols and visits from nature and all the dreams are real. I know you write with me, through me and I suspect you will be communicating through this book. Just know, beautiful daughter, my life has forever been rocked because of you. I can never go back to how it was. It's like a blind person seeing the color green for the first time then trying to un-see it. This whole experience has forever transformed me. Because of it, I am a better person today. All I can say is thank you, thank you, thank you from the huge gaping hole in my heart, thank you.

Journal Entry 12/18/17

I texted Juliana my address, so excited for her to see my new little rental. She will be staying with me for a couple days. After our visit, she will stay at the big house with her father and the rest of the family. It is one week from Christmas and we are expecting to have a few people in for the holidays.

I am planning on spending Christmas in Denver alone and the kids will come up after to celebrate with me.

My ex and I have been separated for almost 9 months and are learning how to split up kid time. The great part about this arrangement is the kids are older.

The day is just an ordinary day in southern Colorado. The weather is mild, a little chilly, no snow yet.

I started out my day in the usual way with a workout and then practice on my aerial equipment. I head home afterwards to take a nap, as I will have rehearsal later in the evening.

It's a little after 1pm and I cannot sleep. My stomach hurts and I'm tossing and turning. I get up thinking I'm hungry but can't manage to eat anything. Something is clearly wrong but I'm not sure what it is.

After hours of trying to rest, I looked at my phone (I keep my phone on silent): 5 missed calls, Malaya and Hunter, and another number. I get up, put on a bathrobe and walk out of my room, calling Malaya back. As the phone was ringing, Malaya came rushing through my door with frantic eyes and a cracking voice. She said, "Mom, something's wrong!"

I asked, "What baby? What?"

She replied, "I don't know; they won't tell me."

That was when I noticed the two police officers standing in my front doorway patiently waiting for me to come down the stairs. My heart sank. The police don't come to my house.

Malaya and I sat on the stairs as the two officers explained that at some time around 1:20 P.M., Juliana drove off a cliff in Wolf Creek Pass and died.

Journal Entry 12/19/17

My daughter Juliana Sunn Ellsmore is dead.

My beautiful 19-year-old sweet Juju baby crashed her car in a canyon and is no more.

Her body is going through an autopsy; she is an organ donor.

My body will not stop shaking.

I had the privilege of spending the last two weekends with her.

Two Fridays ago, I helped her get her driver's license reinstated. She used my truck to take her driver's test.

We drove around Denver looking for an apartment and immediately fell in love with a cute little place close to her school. It felt right. We both knew we wanted to live there. The application process took less than a week and even though neither of us had rental history or work history, we were approved to move in on the 16th.

guess whos back behind the wheel

She was so excited to be moving closer to her school, and we were both looking forward to our adventures of being roommates.

Last Saturday, she and I moved all her stuff from her old apartment into our new one in just a few hours. Alec, her boyfriend, stayed the night, and I woke the two of them bright and early Sunday. I had already ventured out to get us coffee from 7/11. They helped me load my truck. I hugged her tightly knowing I was going to see her the next day. She was staying back to clean and get organized for her trip to Pagosa Springs for the Christmas vacation.

This is all a nightmare. How did I not know that the precious ordinary moments I had with my daughter would be my last? I will never see her gorgeous smile again. I will never hear her loving voice. The huge bear hug she gave me in Denver was the last one. I didn't even get to say goodbye. This cannot be real.

Malaya and I held each other most of the night. I couldn't let her go. My heart was pounding and my breathing labored; tears just keep streaming.

I am waiting for Juliana to come walking through the door calling me Mama. She was such a sweet, wonderful person.

Background

I am a 44-year-old mother of 4 children. My son Hunter was born when I had just turned 21; two years later, I had a daughter Kirra; 15 months later, Juliana was born, and then 2 years after her, Malaya joined the family.

I was a stay-at-home young mother and vowed to raise my kids, as I felt very strongly about keeping my children close. We moved many times, and each of the children was born in a different state.

We had a fun and interesting life of travel, friends and family. Our house was full of visitors and laughter. In the early years, I would pack up all four kiddos and find ways for us to enjoy the town we were living in at the time. I became an

expert in all things free for kids to do, including parks, water fountains, indoor playgrounds, and botanical gardens. The five of us were constantly adventuring out on bikes and strollers with backpacks and lunches packed.

The children were very close; I liked to think of them as my little pack of puppies.

As the kids grew and moved on into school years, they were still very much a unit. All being close in age, they were in the same schools together much of the time. I can only imagine how that must have felt knowing your siblings were so close and had your back.

Fast forward in the middle school ages, we moved to a gorgeous little town in Southern Colorado. The kids were exposed to nature and hiking and camping, fishing and lots of new wonderful friends who became our family.

This little town was a breath of fresh air, as we became a part of the welcoming community.

Each of the children began developing their passions and talents, shining on their own, as individuals.

Juliana had a passion for music and taught herself guitar. She wrote and sang her own songs.

She loved children and worked with children with learning disabilities.

The high school had many great programs to help develop her skills, and she was able to perform for audiences as well as sing on the radio. (Note: I attached her songs to one of my blog posts right after she died. It was listened to over 3500 times.)

One by one, the children moved away. Kirra was off to college in Florida. Hunter moved to California to work and Juliana moved to Denver for massage school. Malaya, our youngest, was in high school and getting very close to graduating.

Darren, the children's father, and I decided to divorce after 23 years of marriage. I moved from our family home and into a tiny rental, taking the steps necessary to create a new life as a single woman. Our family was changing, as all things do. During

this time, Juliana became the family therapist and would call and comfort both of us on a weekly basis. I know this was a beautiful time between her and her father, as they were able to connect on a different level and develop a wonderful friendship. She was a lovely comfort to all of us as we were transitioning into the unknown.

The minutes after Juliana's passing felt like an eternity. Every breath felt like I was at 30 thousand feet with no oxygen. When I would close my eyes, I could only see her. When I would open my eyes, just tears.

My children, my sweet children, were all suffering, and there was nothing I could do to help.

Her poor daddy was so heartbroken and wrecked. All of us were in complete disbelief and shock. I never knew that so much pain was possible. I definitely feared the possibility, but now the feeling was here in the physical. We were all pummeled by the freight train of grief.

Journal Entry 12/19/17

Darren was in Tennessee with his dying father when he got the call of his own daughter's death. I can only imagine the absolute torment and grief he must have felt at the irony of the situation. He immediately jumped on a plane to Colorado.

Kalei, Juliana's half sister, who was planning on staying with her mother's family for Christmas, also made plans to fly to Colorado. Kirra was in Florida, pacing back and forth, knowing she was already scheduled to fly in a couple days. Her fiancé Joe was able to book a ticket and join her in Colorado.

Hunter and Malaya were by my side in my tiny rental, broken and in shock.

Within just a few days of Juliana's death, our family was together, all of us holding on to each other.

Christmas was her favorite holiday, and as she would have it, our family would be joined for the holiday after all.

Journal Entry 12/21/17

Amazing how so much can change in the blink of an eye. Juju has died. Our world has completely flipped upside down. I haven't eaten since Monday. I can't do anything except sit in disbelief staring into nothingness. Today, I was going to drive back to Denver to pick up her stuff, but I will wait till Sunday. It is snowing.

In the end, all that's left is love. There are so many stories of love for Juliana, so many stories about her life, so many memories from her friends and people she touched. She was loved by so many. I still feel like I'll wake up and this will all be a nightmare. Right now, I just sit.

Dear Juliana, dear beautiful, thank you for coming to me. Thank you for choosing me to be your mother. Even in the pain I am feeling right now, I do not regret a single moment. Even in dying, I believe you are connecting me intimately to the next life. I am so grateful I know you are here.

Journal Entry 12/22/17

Pandora (the music app) started playing on my phone. The weird thing is my Pandora is only connected to WIFI and not to cellular; however, it switched on while I was in my car. I didn't recognize the song and couldn't see it on the display. The display was on iTunes and a totally different song. Immediately, I stopped and listened. Later, I looked up the lyrics. The song title was "Maps" (we both have an affinity for maps). the lyrics repeated, "I love you I love you I love you I love you." She's here.

We received a report from the autopsy. Juliana's death was caused by blunt force trauma; her body died on impact. They suspect she fell asleep while driving and her death was immediate. The police had told me there were witnesses and that according to the witnesses and the patterns of the tire track, there was no swerving or breaking, just a straight track. She drove straight off the side of the road and was ejected from the sunroof. Her body had no major lacerations or bleeding, which is an indication of death on impact.

Her body was transported back to Pagosa where we had the opportunity to view her one last lime.

Her body

Darren, Hunter, Kirra, Malaya and I, all together hand in hand, walked slowly into the mortuary anticipating the viewing of our beloved Juliana. After papers were signed and arrangements for her cremation were made, we were escorted into the parlor. She was covered with a blanket, a band around her head covering the incisions made from the autopsy. One arm was placed outside the blanket.

My beautiful daughter, so serene and peaceful, was lying there in front of us. She was perfect, gorgeous like a statue carved in marble. I wanted to shake her and tell her to stop with this sick joke. I wanted her to wake up.

We all stood around in silence, absorbing the reality of her death. I noticed how delicate and beautiful her features were. In life, she was so animated and I had never really taken the time to admire her perfect face.

The arm that was above the covers was the same arm on which she had received her first tattoo. She loved that tattoo and had been drawing it everywhere—on her guitar and schoolbooks, on her wall. She was so proud of her ink.

One by one, we melted into puddles of quivering tears, leaning on each other.

Observing the body was surreal and expansive. I had never seen a dead body, and witnessing my darling daughter's lifeless form was both heart-wrenching and somewhat comforting. She was no longer in that body. That body was just a shell, a vehicle that once carried the essence of Juliana.

We all said our goodbyes. Closure.

Signs

Early that next morning, I was in my little rental, brewing a cup of coffee. I suddenly had the need to look in the drawer of a dresser I had brought over from our family home. I hadn't looked in these drawers before and was curious what was in them. The first thing I found was her favorite pipe. Juliana loved smoking pot and had a favorite pipe shaped like an octopus. The next thing I found was a little black box filled with sparkly jewels. I immediately started laughing and fell to the ground with a handful of diamonds.

I'll explain:

I had gone on a trip to Italy with a girlfriend of mine for her wedding. During the course of our stay, and even during the wedding itself, she kept finding American dimes. Each time she would find a dime, she would cheerfully say, "Oh, that's my grandma." Her grandmother was leaving her little messages from heaven, and she was so delighted to receive them on such an important occasion. Later, when I arrived home, I described this event to my daughters. We all marveled in the communication from the afterlife. We decided then and there we each needed our own form of communication, should one of us die. I jokingly said, "I want you to bring me diamonds, screw dimes."

Little did I know that I would be receiving exactly this from any one any time soon.

Back to the story:

This first sign brought about such a sense of delight and wonder. In that moment I felt so much joy, and I fell on the floor laughing. We had a special way of communicating. She is still here.

Life Celebration

The days felt like a blur; there are so many details to be taken care of when someone passes. Family and friends were starting to arrive.

Our adorable town sent us food and flowers. The entire house was covered in blossoms and bouquets. The three refrigerators were filled with ready-made meals. We began planning for a celebration in her honor.

We had scoured our computers for all pictures of her and printed out over 2500 photos, which we then taped to every wall in the house. Our guests helped cut out paper hearts and ribbon. The hearts were hung from the ceiling, creating a colorful display of dangling love.

I had a very real knowing that Juliana would only want us to celebrate her. She would want us to remember the love and fun memories. She would want us to comfort each other and share her stories. Her death was exactly one week before Christmas, and I had the feeling that this death was affecting so many people in our little community, and we needed to get together before the holidays to say our goodbyes.

Our community, her friends and family needed to move through the holidays with as much love and peace as possible.

Saturday, only five days after her passing.

We opened the house to our town. The newspaper posted an announcement and we used social media to get the word out. Our house was overflowing with love and tears. So many people gathered in her honor. We all wrote little love notes to Juliana and made a huge bonfire to stand around and share our stories and later burn our letters. The home felt like a giant pulsating heart. This girl was deeply loved.

Several pictures were taken during the celebration and many of them contained orbs. Brilliant glowing orbs surrounded us all. There was a picture at the bonfire of a smoky angel floating off in a field. She is all around us.

Sunday, Christmas Eve, Hunter and I drove to Denver towing a trailer with the intentions of cleaning out our cute little apartment. We arrived late in the evening, and with the help of our family friend Paul the entire apartment was packed up in a matter of minutes. Being in the space was surreal, heart breaking and so challenging. In these moments a strange force comes over me and I feel strength in the moving. It's as if my heart turns off for a moment and my body can go into action moving swiftly through the motions. As I was packing some of her clothes my emotions crept in and sideswiped me, I could still smell her on the fabric. I broke down sobbing.

In my teary state I grabbed a box to place the clothes into. Inside the empty box was a diamond earring. I needed to find this exactly at that moment. I wiped away the tears and continued cleaning knowing my sweet daughter was there with me.

We drove home on Christmas morning in a snowstorm. Hunter was peacefully sleeping in the passenger seat, as I was white knuckling the steering wheel through the blizzard. He woke and started changing the radio. He surprisingly said "hey mom did you see that?" I assured him I could only look in front of the truck as I was trying to keep us on the road. He said as he was changing the stations the radio display read, DO NOT SLEEP WHILE SHES DRIVING.

We arrived at the crash spot at the same time and exactly one week after the accident at 1:10 pm. My radio spontaneously changed to a song by Puff Daddy, "I'll Be Missing You," funny thing is it started playing at the chorus.

Every step I take

Every move I make

Every single day

Every time I pray

Ill be missing you

Blog Post Christmas 2017

Thank you all so much for the tremendous outpouring of love and support and compassion and kindness. It has been a nonstop flood of love flowing towards our family. All the food, flowers, gifts and sweet words of comfort have meant so much to our family in this terrible time. We all thank you deeply.

A few words from a mother's perspective.

When I was in labor with Juliana, the midwife told me that natural labor is the most amount of pain a body can handle before it dies. Going through her birth brought a sense of confidence in the knowing that I survived.

However, I believe the midwife was wrong. Feeling the loss and grief over my daughter's death is more. It's not only a physical crippling sensation, it's a literal suffocating fog of the deepest sadness I have ever experienced. It is the worst nightmare materializing and there is not a thing I can do but feel every ounce of excruciating anguish.

What I understand from this experience is pain is nature's tenderizer. It's an opportunity to intimately know the depths of our capabilities. It's also an opportunity to crack wide open and see the other side of love. Once the fire of despair begins to soften, the sweetness of pure love can emerge.

I am feeling that sweet love in so many forms now; I am feeling it in the closeness of our family, in the tender compassion from all our friends and community. I am feeling it in the memories and stories shared. I am feeling it in the beautiful reminders that present themselves in the quiet moments.

I am so incredibly grateful for the precious 19 years of this exquisite girl's life.

My hope for all of you reading this is to not wait to share your love. Hug your kids more, have patience and time for them. Live fully now and know that this life is so temporary.

One more story

A darling little girl told us when she was brought to the site of the crash, "When the time was right, Juliana pressed the button and was gone."

What does this even mean?

My guess is that somehow, there was a knowing that this was her time and she set up her exit, her launching into another plane. Her passing from our world was immediate and painless.

Till we meet again, dear darling.

I promise to make the most of this life with your memory as my inspiration.

As things began to settle down, the quiet sinking feeling of despair began to close in. I was left with so many questions. I wondered how in the world I was ever going to get through this. All I wanted to do was isolate myself, take multiple showers and sleep. My sleepless nights were full of images of the car wreck and her dead cold body.

As much as I wanted to believe she was in a good place, I had a hard time comprehending an afterlife. Where is this afterlife, what does it look like, how can she see without eyes? How can she hear me without ears?

Journal Entry 12/26/17

One week and one day. When is it okay to let go of sadness?

Now! There's no set amount of time you have to feel it. Feel all of it. Let it rip your guts out and then put something beautiful in the new space, a delightful thought or memory or wish for yourself and your life.

I want to know what happens to us when we die. I want to know where my daughter is. I want to intimately know at the core of my being what exactly is waiting for all of us. I do know I am not afraid to die now. My Juju is there waiting for me.

Journal Entry 12/29/17

We went to her car today. The car was in a police wreck yard and an officer assisted us as we went through the remains. I had been looking for a whale tale necklace she purchased on a family vacation in Hawaii. She was so attached to the necklace, she never took it off. I had asked the police and even the coroner about the necklace, and no one had seen it. I decided to climb into the wreckage and dig around the glass fragments. I needed to find this necklace. After searching with no avail, I found a purse. Inside the purse was a journal and an extensive bucket list. What a treasure she wrote a bucket list.

Every corner of this experience I feel a terrible uncertainty.

I feel doubtful in my abilities to make it through and then somehow, I make it through. Somehow, we all step through the experience and make it through. We just do it.

Looking at her dead body, I didn't think I could do it. Touching her cold skin, kissing her forehead, cleaning out the apartment, seeing the car, now climbing through the car—all of it presents itself and I feel doubt and fear and then take a breath and do it anyway.

I'm going to share her bucket list and do my best to complete it in her honor.

Blog Post 12/29/17: Juliana's Bucket List

Thinking about my daughter and her brief 19 years on this planet has given me a new feeling about my own life.

I am so fortunate to have had so many beautiful years with her. Her passing has made me embrace my living children with tremendous love and affection. I have a new respect for all the living beings on this planet and a complete appreciation for how we affect each other's lives. Every life is important and special, and I know we are here to live fully with no regrets.

In the last few weeks of her life, I had the privilege of spending lots of time with her. Together, we found an apartment in Denver. We moved her belongings into our new place, laughed about being schoolgirls and roommates together. We dreamt about our future and all the new possibilities. We talked about how excited she was to graduate from massage school and begin her career. We drank wine from mugs and shared a meatball sub on the couch. Life was so thrilling and bright for her. I know as she was driving home, she was in such a good place mentally and emotionally. I know she was truly happy and full of dreams. She was at a point in her life where everything was looking brilliant and accessible. Her dreams were manifesting daily.

And then that was it, the end.

Her life ended on an exclamation mark.

I know without a doubt that even though her body is no more, she is still here, she is around. She constantly brings little reminders and leads me to look in drawers and books I wouldn't have ever looked in. Music plays at odd times of the day with lyrics that have a message. I have pictures with orbs and ghostly figures. On Christmas morning, the TV turned on by itself, full volume, playing Mariah Carey's "All I Want for Christmas" remix. She loved Christmas. Her father found a piece of her guitar intact with words written in marker, a song he would sing to her every time she would leave for school, "Ain't No Sunshine When She's Gone."

I am finding diamonds everywhere. This was something we agreed upon when she was alive. We jokingly said if either of us dies before the other, we have to bring diamonds to show that we're still here.

We picked up her belongings from the wrecked car and I found her bucket list. She wrote an extensive list of all the things she wanted to experience in her life. She loved to travel and wanted to see the world. I feel like now I have to accomplish these things on her list and bring her ashes with me, spreading a little piece of Juliana all over the world.

Juliana's Bucket List

1. Skydive free fall take the class.
2. Cliff dive.
3. Fall in love.
4. Go to London.
5. Visit Fiji.
6. Visit Jamaica.
7. Carnival in Rio.
8. Para-sail.
9. Wind surf.
10. Have my own concert.
11 Drink in Vegas.
12 Play my French songs in France.

13. Go snowmobiling.

14. Feed a homeless person.

15. Act on TV.

16. Sing on the radio.

17. Paddle board on the Mississippi.

18. Drive a yacht.

19. Go to a frat party.

20. Bungee jump.

21. Slingshot ride.

22. Do a keg stand.

23. Great pyramids Giza.

24. Gardens of Babylon.

25. Statue of Zeus at Olympia.

26. Temple of Artemis.

27. Colossus of Rhodes.

28. Lighthouse of Alexandria.

29. Mausoleum Halicarnassus.

30. Kiss Hugh Jackman.

31. Find and see Luna.

32. Shave my head.

33. Drink 100 beers at Lady Falconburg, family dedicated brick.

34. Live a month in Hawaii.

35. Learn to surf.

36. Take my mom to Spain or somewhere of her choice.

37. Go to Ireland.

38. Meet an Irish lad.

39. Beach bum for a month.

40. Backpack for a month survive the land.

41. Own a farm.

42. Have three kids.

43. Learn to fly a helicopter.

44. Make a scary movie with my mom.

45. Hold a lion cub.

46. Ride an elephant in another country.

47. Kiss Gerard Butler.

48. Learn a new language.

49. Know at least seven languages.

50. Ride a bull.

51. Fall in love with a cop.

52. Fall in love with a cowboy.

53. Fall in love with a tech nerd.

54. Fall in love with a musician.

55. Fall in love with a chef.

56. Fall in love with a traveler.

57. Fall in love with a humanitarian.

58. Fall in love with a Marine or SEAL.

59. Shoot a flaming arrow.

60. Throw a grenade.

61. Set a fire and put it out.

62. Beat up a car.

63. See the northern lights.

64. Date a guy who will join me on this for a while.

65. Spend a night in jail.

66. Get arrested.

67. Talk my way out of being arrested.

68. Fulfill someone's dying wish.

69. Go to Bali.

70. Have a massive food fight.

71. Get this tattoo.

72. Demolish a house.

73. Get into a fight.

74. Learn to hula-hoop.

75. Go on a long romantic horseback ride.

76. Ride the world's largest roller coaster.

77. Have sex in a hospital Grey's style.

78. Start a bar fight.

79. Break a bottle on someone's head.

80. Meet a monkey.

81. Visit India.

82. Visit Japan.

83. Audition to whatever in Hollywood.

84. Go to Moulin Rouge.

85. Screw a British bloke.

86. See the northern lights.

87. Go to Niagara Falls.

88. See 21 Pilots.

89. See Red Hot chili Peppers.

90. Ride a dog sled.

91. Stay in Alaska for a year.

92. See Russia.

93. Fly a plane.

94. Get married.

Journal Entry 12/30/17

Something really cool just happened. Another message from Juliana. Earlier in the day, I had run up to the family house and went into the trailer containing all of Juliana's belongings from the apartment. I picked up a couple things wanting to find more journals or artwork, maybe songs. Basically, anything and everything now had meaning. I randomly grabbed a canister. It was old metal and looked like a worth-

less piece of trash. When I got to my rental, I opened the canister and sure enough, the first thing that fell out was the whale tale necklace. This was an incredible find. A miracle she never took the necklace off and somehow it found its way in a bizarre canister filled with junk jewelry. I immediately called her daddy. All I asked was if he was at the house, then I said, "Stay there. I have something for you."

He needed the necklace, and as soon as I touched it, I saw his face in the back of my mind, knowing this find was for him.

Chapter 2
January

Journal Entry 1/4/18

I'm working on Juliana's bucket list. The idea of accomplishing so many fun tasks makes me feel like I have a purpose. I started with language and am learning French, Portuguese, Italian and Spanish. Really I'm just learning the Prayer of St. Francis and translating it line by line.

Hey Mama. Yes, baby, I love you. How is it?

Fun!

I bet. What are you working on?

Everything.

How can I help our family?

Get through first, write, play, laugh.

What about your dad?

He'll be fine.

Do you have any messages for anyone?

LOVE LOVE LOVE LOVE LOVELOVELOVELovelovelovelovelovel ovelovelovelovelovelovelovelovelovelovelovelovelovelov elovlovelovelovelovelove

What does that even mean?

Kindness, acts of service, sharing, generosity, allowing, accepting. I come through other people.

Journal Entry 1/6/18

My throat is closed. I cannot eat. I looked it up in Louise Hay's book about metaphysical meanings to physical issues. It states the throat is the avenue of expression, the channel of creativity. Inability to speak up, swallowed anger, stifled creativity, refusal to change.

Yesterday, I gave Kirra some of Juliana's ashes. There were bone chunks in it and some of the ashes were on my skin. I felt the creepy reality that my daughter's body was burned. She was cremated and all that remains are these ash specks on my skin, dust and bone in my throat and it's closing up.

This may take some time. My body is grieving the loss. It's going through withdrawals of being a mother. My cells are learning to let go. In my mind and heart, I know she's ok, but my body keeps shaking, crying and feeling sad.

Life is for living, dreaming, playing and creating. The dead assist and are not dead, just not in bodies. They help create by prompting us to do things, say things, and go places.

Journal Entry 1/8/18

I am alone. The whirlwind of people has subsided and I am quietly alone in my little rental, looking at the police report. It gives detailed forensic accounting: the distance the car launched, how many times it rolled, where her body landed. I still expect her to walk through the door with a huge smile and a cheerful greeting of, "Hey Mama." I miss those words. I miss her. I've been looking for clues, in people and pictures, even in old journal entries. I wonder if some part of me knew this was about to happen. She was always going to die on that day. Was there something I missed?

Journal Entry 1/9/18

I went back to work. I taught the morning CrossFit classes then headed home exhausted. My dreams were intense. Dreams within dreams, and each time I tried to wake, I was still in a dream. I finally woke and began violently throwing up. My body felt like it was shutting down. I continued to puke and shit my guts out for the rest of the day. The only place that felt safe was my shower. I spent hours in the shower screaming. I am so tired and sore.

My body is letting her go. I am squeezing her out of every pour. I am releasing the physical attachment. I'm sure this has to do with the fact that we shared this damn body and it doesn't want to let go. It is fighting me, ripping my heart out and clogging my mind. This body is battling to simply let go.

Giant boulders are crushing me, and I'm afraid there will be nothing left of me when this pain subsides, if it ever will.

I had a vision of swimming in a black tumultuous sea with waves as high as buildings. I panic and want to give up. I let the water take me. I sink in the darkness. Then something miraculous happens: I realize I have the power to make a boat, a life-saving vessel. It is constructed of all the pictures and memories of my sweet daughter's life, of her love. I climb aboard and am safe. The waves are still crashing, but now I have a way to ride above them.

Blog Entry 1/9/18: Clues

The Sunday before her accident, I was with her in Denver getting ready to drive to Pagosa. As I was leaving, she handed me a friend's skateboard and said, "Please make sure he gets it." At first, I thought it was a little weird that she wanted me to take it because she would be driving down the next day. Needless to say, the skateboard was delivered safely. She never made it.

During my drive home, as I was winding through the canyon that she would die in, I randomly thought, "This would be a good canyon to die in; all you have to do is drive straight."

As most of you know, that's exactly what happened to Juliana. She just drove straight off a cliff.

She wore a whale tale necklace from Hawaii every day. She never took it off. After the accident, I was asking about the necklace, but neither police nor the coroner had seen a necklace. Later, as I was going through some of her things, I just happened upon a container of jewelry her necklace was inside.

She wrote a song telling us to "smile" and "please don't forget my love," that "life is worth it, 'cause you are so precious to me."

A few months ago, I wrote a post about diving off a cliff, sailing towards the "one finale."

I also had a vivid dream about swapping skin suits and when I was finished with the suit I could leave it by causing a heart attack, a car wreck, or cancer.

In the summer I had an experience of leaving my body and what it feels like to be on the other side. I think this was a necessary experience for my understanding and ability to process the death of my 19-year-old daughter.

I look for her everywhere. When scouring over pictures taken with her friends, I see her. In the dimly-lit room, I see flickers of something. I hear her in my head saying, "Hey Mama," then we have quiet conversations about life.

I still miss her deeply. I'm sure the feelings will continue as I loved her deeply. The physical attachment is so strong. For the past 24 hours, I've been puking and sleeping. I believe this is my body's way of letting her go.

For now, this is it. I know that in time, all this will change as everything in life does eventually change. But until then, I will continue to search for clues that she is still here with us, clues that she is communicating her love to us. Clues that we are so much more than we think and that death is just another part of living.

Journal Entry 1/11/18

Something has shifted. I must be going crazy. As I sit and stare out my window, my vision has changed. It is as if the lenses of my eyes have pulled back and there is a gap between my vision and my actual eyes. Within the gap is black space filled with a "behind the scenes" crew of people. They're all hustling around trying to get my sight back on track but cannot. I can see everything that is actually going on as well as the world my eyes are picking up. It's a peek into the workings of the beyond and my misperception. Juju is here. She looks like a shadow but I recognize her essence.

There is so much more to this life than what my eyes are picking up.

Journal Entry 1/14/18

I have been dissecting my beliefs one by one, asking if they actually make any sense or if I just believe them because I always have.

I realized that beliefs are a unique force in nature that causes things to happen. They literally are the beginning point of all creation. What's fascinating about them is they can change according to what we want to experience, but only if we believe so.

Beliefs are the mental program running the show. They even run the behind the scenes and are so ingrained in everything, we cannot see them unless we start to question our world. When we realize that we create the beliefs in the first place, we put ourselves at the helm of the ship. We begin to run our ship as we please, and we use the mental program for our benefit.

I believe we are made up of energy, and energy by definition cannot be destroyed; it can only be transformed. Therefore, when we die, it is only our bodies that die but our energy continues.

I believe the part of us that is causing the human fleshy body to walk around is our energy self, and it is always connected to something bigger. We are all connected to this bigger something.

I believe we have many abilities that can be developed, including communicating with those who may not have bodies.

I believe I can communicate with my angel daughter.

I believe there are no accidents.

Journal Entry 1/16/18

I'm thinking about my life as a mother. Of course I wonder if I did a good job, if I did enough with the time I had. Did I make a difference in my children's lives? Did I love them enough? Was I open and caring? Did I teach them to be loving, wonderful people and to love themselves? Did they know they were cherished beyond measure? Did Juliana know?

My work as a mother was long and tedious and delightful and wondrous and not long enough.

I didn't really give it any thought or choice; I just did it every day, every moment, morning, day and night. It was never a question; I was just mom. Everyone said, "They grow too fast." Now I am one of the warning moms saying to treasure their moments. They do grow too fast and die too soon.

It's strange being at the beginning and the end of a life. I was always there for her, but she was just a short blip for me.

I had been writing daily, mostly to process what was carving away at my existence. I would use my early morning meditation and writing sessions to make sense of my world. I started posting on a blog right after Juliana died and noticed my posts were being read thousands of times (I still only have 2 followers).

Juliana's death had rocked so many lives. People who didn't even know her were reaching out to me, sending their love and condolences.

I wanted to share this rocky path, knowing that at some point we all get to walk it. My hope was that in finding some peace I could offer peace.

After the post about her bucket list, I was given a beautiful offer to stay in Puerto Rico with a sweet friend of mine. She had read the bucket list and wanted to help us mark a few things off: surfing and cliff diving.

I took the offer. Malaya and I jumped on a plane and flew to Florida. We made it just in time for Kirra's 21st birthday (which was a spontaneous delightful surprise to all of us). During the party, there was a picture taken of the three of us, and a very clear blue orb on Kirra's belly. We started looking for the orb in all our pictures.

When we arrived on the island, the blue orb came with us; it showed up in our first video of driving.

The Island of Puerto Rico was in recovery. They had been hit by a massive hurricane a few months prior and were putting their world back together. What a perfect place for us to be to gain some perspective. (The world just keeps spinning and the sun comes up every day, like it or not.)

Journal Entry 1/26/18

In Puerto Rico, Malaya and I have been staying with my sweet friend and her two kids in their adorable house overlooking the ocean. Rincon is a gorgeous surf spot with tall cliffs and epic waves.

This home is peaceful and filled with nature's white noise. Roosters, birds, dogs, crickets, twirls, whistles and chirps. So much life here and it seems to move with a gentle rhythm.

I'm currently enjoying a sweet cup of coffee alone on the deck. It is early and the morning breeze is refreshing. I cherish my alone times, my quiet connecting moments. I have wanted to dive into this solace more and more. I have so many moments of missing my Juliana and realize I would not be right here if it were not for her. She is the reason I am on this gorgeous island. I am excited to continue with her bucket list. I love the feeling of living more fully because she wanted to. Today, we will go cliff diving; tomorrow, surfing. I will bring along some of her ashes to spread in the water.

Looking at a picture of Juliana, I wonder what she looks like now. Where is she? How can I see her? I want to know. Honey, where are you?

I'm right here. (The dog just came and sat next to me.)

You just brought Rouka (the dog) to me, didn't you?

Yes.

Oh baby, I feel so much it's hard to describe. I want to keep my energy high so I can experience you. My feelings are like giant waves of emotion. I'm having a hard time controlling them. What can I do to see you?

Open up more, see more, look with your heart not your eyes.

 What do you look like?

Everything.

There's a pressure in my physical heart. It feels like ripping muscles; it makes my eyes cry and my breathing restricted.

Sensation isn't pain. It's part of being in a body.

I'm bringing your ashes with us today.

Give them to Malaya.

Ok.

Later that day, we drove to San Sebastian and hiked to a waterfall. I jumped off the cliff, knowing my daughter was right there with me. Malaya and I hiked up a little further and launched her ashes off the edge, and wouldn't you know it, the ashes blew right into our faces. I believe this is Juliana's way of playing with us.

The next day, Malaya took surf lessons and paddled out with some ashes. We also tossed a handful into the ocean, standing on the shore, and even though the wind was blowing out to sea, the ashes blew right into Malaya's face again.

Journal Entry 1/28/18

Our last day in PR; it's been wonderful. The water here has been healing, and our friends have been amazing tour guides. We both thoroughly enjoyed our brief stay and definitely want to come back. Juliana showed up in my dream; she was standing in a doorway with ripped jean shorts and a white T-shirt. Her hair was in a messy pile on the top of her head and she was smiling.

Chapter 3
February

We have a few days in Florida to visit with friends and share stories of our travels. The girls decide to do the "SlingShot" and bring along some of Juliana's ashes. They launched the ashes at 400 feet in the air. Bucket list item #21 complete.

Journal Entry 2/4/18

We are back in Denver. We stayed at Paul's house last night and will drive home to Pagosa today. I woke to a heavy fog covering his entire property. I watched the fog settle and expose a lucent azure morning sky.

My dreams are so vivid and colorful. I have been writing them down religiously; they generally don't make too much sense but I suspect with practice, I will be able to see the connections and symbols of communication to the other world.

I am writing in Juliana's journal. I finished my last one in PR and just happened to have her diary with me. I found this book in her wrecked car; she only wrote a few pages, so I will fill these pages.

The cover of the book states "LIVE A LIFE FULL OF INCREDIBLE ADVENTURES AND EMBRACE THE JOURNEY." A sign? I am taking this sign to heart. I think about all the amazing adventures that have already been lived.

I have a new sense of wanting to continue to create a beautiful, exciting, wondrous life. I feel the fog of depression lifting and what is left is a new brilliant view. I am seeing with eyes of possibility. I want to take the time I have left and love and laugh and sing and dance my way through it. I want to learn how to communicate more clearly with my daughter and share with the world. I am so curious. I want to know what it's like for her. I know she is there, here, everywhere all the time. I want to know what that is like.

Pagosa

Arriving back into my life and immediately going to work, staying busy with my newfound focus, the bucket list. I practice my language daily and study and begin creating swimwear with my daughter Malaya. The days pass with gratitude, having an optimistic mindset.

I still waver back and forth between emotions of despair and delight. I feel like a crazy person, or maybe a manic-depressive.

The underlying question is, when will this all feel ok? The answer I'm getting is eventually I will learn to live with this. Faith is the gap between belief and reality. I must have faith that it will all be ok, and then it will be.

Journal Entry 2/14/18

I made an appointment to speak with a medium. This will be my first time communicating with a person who talks to spirits. I'm really excited to hear what she has to say. I am also planning a snowboarding trip with Malaya and Hunter. I am so lucky to have such great kids.

Journal Entry 2/17/18

I can't sleep; I keep seeing car accidents when I close my eyes. My mind is in such a state of worry and fear. Why is my mind behaving this way?

Blog Post 2/17/18

I can't sleep.

What is going on, what am I to do with myself?

I feel an overwhelming dark cloud of grief and worry swirling around me.

My thoughts are of my children and their safety, of how I need to keep them safe and literally cannot.

Their lives are their own, and I am here as a witness.

I get to marvel in their world but it does not belong to me.

Nothing belongs to me.

My fear has got a hold of my thoughts and is twisting my perception to one of despair, anguish, anxiety and torment.

I decide to get out of bed. I need to do something other than flip and flop in my sleepless state.

I sit in the shower; the warm water feels soothing on my skin. I make my way down stairs for a cup of tea and my journal.

Somehow, I know I can work this out in writing.

Writing has helped in so many ways. It seems that when the thoughts are translated into words on paper, I can make sense of them.

Here's what I came up with.

I am currently going through grief. It's a given and to be expected when losing someone special. This is something every person will go through at some point. Loss is a part of living and loving.

My daughter's sudden death will continue to reverberate through my cells and take me when I least expect it. And it's all ok. It's ok to feel vulnerable and weak. It's ok to feel sorrow and heartache.

It's ok to sit quietly in my pajamas and stare at the walls.

Its ok to feel all of it and let the emotion work its way through me.

I also understand that my new feelings of fear are directly related to feeling powerless and helpless around the death of my daughter. There was absolutely nothing I could do to make anything any different.

I couldn't save her.

I couldn't be there for her when she left this world.

I couldn't tell her I loved her, wish her well, or say goodbye.

What I worked out on paper is this:

None of us know when we will take our last breath. The thoughts that torture me are only thoughts, and the reality of the situation is I am here now.

My children are here now; they are safe now and happy now.

They are healthy and excited about their lives.

My fear will only infect them to play it safe, to live smaller, easier, simpler lives. When in truth, I want the world for them.

I want these beautiful people to know their true power and to live with all their hearts.

I want them to boldly go into the world and love every minute of their creation, no matter how long or short it may be.

I practice breathing, I sip my tea, I write to you and now I can sleep.

Being home in Pagosa was bittersweet. I did my best to stay busy and focus on accomplishing what I could, considering the bucket list. As the days passed, I began to get irritated and edgy. My emotions were running away with me. There was also the feeling of not wanting to be social. I know our little community was all still very raw, and I felt that everywhere I would go would bring about memories and emotions and tears. The people I would speak with were all so loving but I could tell my presence was making them feel uncomfortable. Dealing with the death of a loved one is challenging, especially a young person. Everyone I knew was taking this to heart and feeling so many unbearable emotions.

After a few days of being home, I just wanted to leave.

Hunter, Malay and I drove to Utah. I was so happy to be spending time with these two. We went snowboarding at Snowbird and stayed with some of our closest friends.

When we arrived at our friend's house, an amazing thing happened.

I had brought them some of Juliana's ashes, and as I was talking to them about the ashes, I felt a little pinch in the leg of my pants. I unconsciously stood up mid-sentence and reached in my leggings and pulled out a diamond (rhinestone). We all stared in disbelief. I had just driven 8 hours with this rhinestone in my pants and hadn't noticed.

This family was Juliana's second family; the girls grew up together and the parents loved her like their own. She adored the Nelsons and of course would want to show them she's there with them.

Chapter 4

March

3/15/18: Juliana's Birthday

On this day, she would have been 20. The day started out dreary with gray skies and a cold drizzle. We were planning on gathering at the lake and releasing 20 purple balloons into the sky. The weather would be a factor as no one wanted to go out in the wet cold.

The gathering was scheduled for 1pm and surprisingly, the weather cleared enough for our party to continue. Several people showed up, bringing flowers and balloons.

There were hugs and tears and music and of course pot smoking in her honor. When the time came to release the balloons, the sky cleared even more and we watched all the balloons make their way past trees without popping and into the open blue sky, all staying together.

What a tough day.

I was feeling a tremendous amount of gratitude for all the people who continued showing up and supporting us through these moments.

The day after her birthday, she would have graduated from massage school. Juliana's father and I were invited to accept her diploma in her stead. She had worked so hard for this diploma.

In the few weeks prior to her passing, she had left school to visit with her dying grandfather in Tennessee. Her week off of school put her behind and she had to make up all the work to finish on time. Her days were long and tedious. I know she was tired.

It seems in the big picture of things that if Juliana were to depart this world on the day she did, then several other things would have had to play a factor. Driving to Pagosa was a long drive, but she had made it so many times, she knew the road well. However, the combination of preparing for graduation, studying for finals, making up lost school days, and driving the 5 hours home all added up for one perfectly timed disaster, her exit point.

Sleep is a good way to go.

(At least that is what I tell myself in order to be ok with it.)

Blog Post 3/23/18: Words from a Medium

As most of you know, my beautiful 19-year-old daughter passed away just a few months ago. She was in a tragic car accident and died (according to the coroner), immediately on impact. The last few months have been so challenging to navigate. I have been searching for comfort and understanding and made an appointment with a psychic medium. It took 6 weeks to talk with her, and I am happy I did. Here are some of the words that came through. Enjoy.

Note: The woman has an adorable Australian accent and some of her expressions didn't make sense, but I wrote them anyway.

Who's lost a child? I hear someone say, "I'm her child." Have you got one in heaven?

—Yes—

Your girl is well, yet she went tragically.

She also said you didn't have time to say goodbye to her.

— No—

So she's come in today to tell you all about everything, ok.

There's a birthday coming up? I hear happy birthday.

— She just had her birthday—

You all were around for her birthday? She's showing me roses all around the place. How old was she?

She's beautiful.

—She was 19—

Beautiful, she showed me her hair, she's slick in her hair. She said to tell you she's dancing with the angels.

Also, she said you'll never get rid of her. She lives with the other kids as well. Every time you look at one of them, you'll see there mannerisms or you'll see her looks in somebody else. Then you'll see somebody walking like her. She said, "Mom, you'll never get rid of me."

—OH, great I love that —

She's in your heart, and have you got her bracelet, earrings or anything? She said you've got little pieces of hers.

She said, "One minute I was here, the next minute I was gone; no time to say goodbye." Is that right?

—Yes—

She said she didn't even see that coming.

—Oh my, ok—

She said all she remembers is one minute she's here and the next thing "I'm in the light."

Something about parent figures, grandfather on the other side.

Grandparents helped her over.

There's a lovely father figure there who helped her.

So, you're really in horrible grief?

—It comes and goes—

You'll never get over it, you know, but you'll learn to live with it. Your daughter, she did give you a run for your money.

—Ha yes, she did—

She said, "I was a hand full." She said she didn't realize till she went over to the other side. She said she couldn't believe how many people paid tribute to her.

—Wow—

"Yeah, I didn't realize how many people knew me or knew of me," she said,

"I just couldn't believe it."

—That's great—

She's showing me balloons.

—Yes, we all just let go of balloons for her birthday—

She said she was in heaven catching them.

You'll never get rid of her, I'll tell you that.

She's with you forever. She's saying she's so sorry. She's so sorry that she left the way she did. She's so sorry and so sorry for you know all the things she used to do. She says she realized.

On the other side, she will teach young kids; she'll play with them and teach them to dance to be happy and that's the nature of us.

Who found her?

—It was an accident; there were two witnesses —

There was help there but it was too late. And also that accident, she said she didn't see that coming. Did she hit a pole or skid? Oh ok, she said she didn't see it coming; was it dark?

She didn't commit suicide.

—No, we think she was sleeping—

She said again, "I wasn't aware."

Those words, her words, "I wasn't aware. I didn't see it coming." Help came but it was too late.

—Yes—

She can't remember much about it. She wouldn't remember if she was asleep.

One minute she was here and the next minute she was in the light.

That accident, she woke up to the light; that's all she remembers.

—I'm glad she didn't have to feel it —

She went the way she lived.

She was a good girl.

Who's a nurse or a teacher?

—Not sure—

Did she have friend whose gone into nursing or teaching?

You need to keep talking about her and encourage others to keep talking about her; she didn't live to be forgotten.

Too big an enterprise.

She was fun there.

She really was.

She said she couldn't believe how many people paid tribute to her, she couldn't believe the memorial. You must have had a memorial or you must have had another party for her.

Something about the beach?

Why is she talking about the beach?

—I took some of her ashes to the beach—

That's what she's trying to tell me. "I'm on the beach." She must have loved going to the beach, that's for sure.

She said, "I'm everywhere." She must be everywhere.

—Yeah—

You must have put her in a few places or people have gotten her ashes.

She said, "I'm spread out."

—We've been sharing her, yes—

She loved music. She liked to dance, she really did and she liked kids, as well, you know.

—Yes—

Were some of her friends going to be nurses or going into the medical field?

She liked dancing, she liked to go out you know with friends and stuff.

She did like nice clothes.

Is one of her sisters a few years older than her? And has she got a boyfriend?

Your daughter is telling me she has, she seems to be saying, "'Bout time they got something sorted." (Giggling)

Whether or not they're living together or making plans but

that relationship will either make or break her in the next year or two.

Do you like him?

—Do I like him? Oh yes I do—

She said if Mom likes him, he's past the test.

She said he's all right.

Tell your daughter safe sex.

She said when you do become a grandmother, she'll hold that baby's spirit before it comes here. She'll know when the time is right and she said safe sex; she doesn't want any of them having children yet.

I can see in the next couple years a wedding, someone moving house?

— You see a house? —

Yes, someone's talking about buying a house.

Is that 3 bedrooms?

I can see a pale color blue.

—Yes, Kirra just bought a house and is engaged to be married—

You are wearing something belonging to your daughter as your speaking to me?

You got a tattoo?

— Ha, I do have a tattoo and it is funny, as you spoke, I put my hand on it—

Yes, she said you wear it on your heart and she said don't get any more, tell them all not to get any more, it's fine. Fine with her.

Who's called Kalei? You'll hear from her now, your daughter said she's all right.

And who's got the A name?

—Alyssa? —

Ok

I saw a big A; who is Alyssa?

—Alyssa is Julianas best friend—

Ahh, she must be going through hell as well cuz she's also getting a rose.

Yeah, your daughter loves everybody. They may not have thought it when she was here, but she certainly can see that she loved all her family, she still does.

She's with grandparents.

Were you close to your grandmother on your mum's side? She has really nice hair.

She said she's met up with your daughter, and they're getting on like a house on fire.

How's your husband? How's her dad?

—He's having a hard time —

He loves his girls; he loves his family. And you need to tell him she's at peace and she's made a good passing and she didn't suffer. Cuz his mind is taking over.

She couldn't believe how many boys paid tribute to her as well.

And had she got a diploma or a certificate from school?

—Yes—

She said she was there and said, "I wouldn't have missed that for the world."

She loved music, she liked the arts as well; she was creative.

Who draws? Who's the architect? Are you thinking of doing plans around the house or making it bigger?

Are you playing her music?

—Yes—

She said you are, she said, "Guess what, they're all playing my music.'"

Ahhh, she's fun that one.

She's entertaining the angels, that's for sure, and dancing with them.

They used to say in the old days only the good die young and those young beautiful people who die are angels now.

And you know, they always give you a run for your money.

They're always larger than life.

And they're still around you. She'll always be around you and when you pass over, which you're not going anywhere yet you'll meet your daughter exactly the same before she passed over.

She's more beautiful; she's really more glittery.

And so you keep your head up, keep yourself busy.

Losing a child and going through a divorce at the same time is horrible.

But you have to go through things.

It takes twelve months to get your head together after the death of a child; it takes two years really to know what you're doing.

You've gotta just take it one step at a time for the next six to twelve months.

After speaking with the medium, I had a feeling of confirmation. A profound knowing that all the things we were experiencing were real. My daughter was still here and doing her best to communicate with all of us.

I also had a feeling of letting go of some of my personal pressure. I had been battling with myself to just get over it. However, in the conversation, I felt a sense of relief and a permission to take my time. I was in a life upheaval and in no way ready to make any serious moves.

I decided the best thing I could do was get some perspective. Separate myself from the immediate situation and surroundings and continue with my course of education. Needing to put the puzzle pieces of my life in some sort of order. I had a divorce coming up and no real course of action to take as far as a career was concerned.

I packed up once again and drove to Florida. I needed to continue working on my ratings as a pilot so I could work professionally once my divorce was finalized.

I stayed with my friend Sue and her family in their home for two full months and was able to work diligently on my flying.

Chapter 5
April

Journal Entry 4/28/18

I finished writing in Juliana's journal. It's wild how the words just flow and the pages fill. I am so grateful to have this form of expression, especially at this time. There is so much inside of me, I feel like I will burst. Life is wonderful and confusing and being so full of all these emotions is sometimes overwhelming.

Today, I feel really good. I am in Florida staying with a dear friend and her family. They have agreed to host me for two months while I focus on my flight training.

I am happy to have a challenge to commit my attention to. One of the flight self-assessments has us evaluate our emotional stability. I think I'll keep that one to myself; I wouldn't want anyone to know that I'm riding a grief rollercoaster daily.

The truth is I'm happy to have a focus. Time is going to pass regardless of what I'm doing, so I might as well be doing something productive and consuming. Flying is a way to take my mind off of the loss of my daughter, even if it is just temporary.

I'm wearing Juliana's dress. I love wearing her clothes. This is the dress she wore when we took a trip to southern California for her 18th birthday. She looked so beautiful in it. I have many pictures of her prancing around on the beach playing with the water. She was a delightful girl, so spunky and fun. Her smile would light up the room and warm anyone's heart. God, I miss her.

I'm so grateful we had the opportunity to create such wonderful memories. Our road trip to California was filled with memories. We drove straight from Pagosa Springs, Colorado to Huntington Beach, California, in one day then spent the next five days exploring southern California. I took her to San Diego where she was born, and reminded her of the story of her birthday when I was walking along the shore in La Jolla and pet a baby seal. This is part of her birth story; she believed I went into labor because I pet a baby seal.

We made it a point to ride as many rollercoasters as we could and were able to ride all the major rollercoasters at Magic Mountain thanks to the fast pass. (I tell you, the extra money was so worth it.) She wanted to perform at an open mike night and as fate would have it, she was invited to sing in the hotel we stayed at spontaneously. We had a chance to visit with my sister and her family and she again pulled out the guitar and jammed with the boys.

I love you, Juliana! *I love you, Mama*! I know. I hope you're having so much fun!

Journal Entry 4/29/18

Juliana's death is teaching me so much about myself. I'm learning to ask in every moment, "What is it I really want?"

"What is most important to me in this exact moment?" "How do I want to feel?" The most helpful mantra is, "This is all temporary." My mind likes to feel sad and sorry for myself, and in these moments, I ask for help. I'm learning to trust in the unseen guidance, in my soul teachers and in guides and now in my daughter. I love that every once in a while, I hear a little something and know, without a doubt, she is communicating her love.

Journal Entry 4/30/18

I'm at my daughter's house; Kirra is a beautiful young lady and a fantastic hostess. She has taken great care to make me feel comfortable and loved. I'm studying and have been for hours. I took a little break and chose to lie on the ground. I rested by the pool and looked up into the clear blue sky. I said quietly, "God, are you there?" Suddenly, a wind picked up and blew the pool float across the pool and onto the deck just a few feet away from me. I sat up and laughed out loud, surprised by the immediate response. I lay back down with a huge smile on my face and then said, "Is that all you got?" I then noticed a rather large millipede crawling on my neck. I jumped up and screamed and said, "Thank you, I'm good."

Chapter 6
May

Journal Entry 5/1/18

Today while Kirra and I were relaxing on the couch, we decided to take a selfie. As soon as I pointed the phone at us, it turned off. She took her phone out and her phone did the same thing. When I rebooted my phone, there were several random pictures on my phone that I hadn't taken: pictures of the ground outside.

Kirra told me her phone acts up constantly and she thinks its Juliana, and sometimes, she yells at her sister out loud to stop. It has even happened to her fiancé Joe, and he has also said out loud to Juliana to please stop messing with his phone.

That day, the TV was acting up and shutting off and then after it was restarted, there was a picture on the screen with Juliana's written name along the bottom right side of the screen. We took a picture of the screen and the phone screen displayed the words (Camera Error, the camera device encountered a fatal error).

Juliana is playing with our electric equipment. She must be having fun trying to get our attention.

Thanks JUJU, I love you, baby!

I love you too, MAMA!

Journal Entry 5/3/18

We are in New Orleans. Malaya is with me. We came here to celebrate her 18th birthday. I love this city; something about it feels so raw and venerable and magical. I am happy to share this place with Malaya. I brought some of Juliana's ashes with us. On her bucket list, she wrote that she wanted to paddleboard the on the Mississippi River. I wonder if we can make this happen. I'll do my best.

Journal Entry 5/5/18

Yesterday was Malaya's birthday. We had a fun day exploring the city, taking pictures, trying the local food, and of course, having coffee and beignets at Café Du Monde. Then something happened and her mood shifted. She broke down completely, sobbing uncontrollably. Remembering her sister and that Juliana was the best at celebrating birthdays. She would usually wake Malaya up first thing in the morning and have something spectacular planned for her.

On her 16th, she filled her car with balloons at the high school parking lot then proceeded to celebrate with Malaya by getting her drunk. Malaya's breakdown had us in tears and laughter. I believe these moments of supreme emotion come to remind us of our love, of the tremendous love we shared. We finished the evening by dressing in pjs, eating chicken Alfredo and of course having a gigantic chocolate dessert covered in whipped cream.

Journal Entry 5/8/18

I had a very clear realization today. Juliana is with me more now than she ever could have been when she had a body. Now I can bring her on all my trips and excursions. She gets to fly with me in the helicopter and sit with me in the quiet mornings. We are still so connected. I love knowing this.

I feel extremely connected to all my children and am so lucky to be a mother of four lovely people, even if one of the four does not have a body.

I want to get better at communicating with my angel daughter.

I am reminded to cherish my moments with my living children and send them love whenever I think of them.

Journal Entry 5/15/18

It's early, 6am. I'm sitting on the couch in Sue's house. It's quiet; no one is up yet. I absorb the scenery. Her giant glass doors open out onto a pool deck and then expand out to a beautiful river. The water is glassy calm; the sky is changing to brilliant streaks of pink and orange. The fish jump every once in a while, and I wonder why the fish jump. I hear "for fun." I want to believe that. Why do any of us do what we do? My mind feels clear and peaceful. I am settling into a calm rhythm and know that all the emotional turmoil is temporary. The main emotion I feel in this moment is gratitude. All of life is amazing and miraculous.

Blog Post 5/22/18: Check In

I'm currently sitting in a little white, well-lit room on a comfy bed. My bags and books are all around me. I will be diving into my studies in a bit, but I just wanted to get a few words out as they are coming to me now.

I have been in South Florida for almost seven weeks and have been staying with a sweet family who have opened their home to me. I came here to get a change of perspective. I came here with the intention of working on my flying so eventually I can work as a professional helicopter pilot. I'm still very inexperienced and still have so much work to do. I love flying. I love learning and at this point in my life, I'm so grateful I have it as a distraction.

Before I chose to come here, I was basically isolating myself from the world, submerged in the depths of my own grief and heartache. I would spend my days sitting on the couch, staring at the walls, completely lost, not knowing how to navigate my own heart and the feelings of losing my child.

Being here has caused a tremendous shift. I have been up every day before sunrise. I have been studying non-stop and flying as much as I can. Working on becoming an instrument-rated pilot has taken so much work and focus. These new skills are challenging and take so much of my mental capacity. I have been able to put my loss in the background of my mind and dedicate my wandering thoughts to learning. There is a lot involved when trying to fly a helicopter with only reference to instruments. The information alone is astounding. It is a whole new language, and I am happy to challenge my 44-year-old brain with this new task.

Many times throughout the days, I have asked myself what I'm really doing here. Why am I making myself take on this major task? What is it I'm trying to accomplish?

My answer is, I'm not really sure. I just needed something to shift my world and help me get moving in a healthy direction.

What I'm realizing is I needed to open up and let other people in. I needed to put myself in a place where I had to talk to people. Living with this gracious family has made me open up and share love. I do miss my own family. I adore my children and miss them terribly.

I have had the privilege of visiting with my daughter who lives here in Florida. What a treat; she is a beautiful person with a blossoming life, and being in her presence is inspiring. I also had the great opportunity to meet my 18-year-old daughter in New Orleans to celebrate her 18thbirthday. We had so much fun in the city, and I felt so grateful to have spent some time with her. She too is such an amazing individual and is growing into the most gorgeous, loving person.

I wish I could have my son come visit, but I will be home soon enough and can't wait to see him.

I am so proud of these people and feel incredibly lucky that I get to be their mother.

Every day is a new challenge. I have to wake up and remind myself this life is a gift and having a heart that feels so deeply is something I want to experience.

I feel like our time here is a brief journey into the realm of feeling and contrast and creation.

My daughter's death has opened me up to a whole other side of life. I have had some magical moments where I know without a doubt she is still here.

She is present in our lives and is cheering for us to find love and fulfillment. She walks with us throughout the daily tasks, showing her love in any way possible. I feel she is doing her best to remind us in every moment that there is so much more to this existence. There is a whole invisible world of assistance and love always watching.

I think she is the one who gave me the quiet inspiration to get my butt off the couch and take some time in Florida to get my head straight.

I feel like she whispers to me when I feel overwhelmed and encourages me to keep going. I feel like she's with me right now typing this post so I can share with you, with all of you who loved her.

I know that at some point, my experience of her death will help others open to their loved ones who have transitioned.

This life is a spectacular journey of feeling emotions that expand our beings, and being here is our choice.

All of it!

Chapter 7
June

Journal Entry 6/1/18

I had a dream with Juliana; the texture of this dream felt more real than any dream I've ever had.

Juliana came to me and said she wanted to show me something. She and I walked down a long corridor and through a doorway. In the darkened room was a large screen playing the movie of Juliana's possible life scenarios.

As this drama unfolded, I witnessed Juliana's three exit points. One when she was 15 (which would have been suicide), and another when she was 19 (car accident). The final exit point was much later in life but would have caused more pain than she wanted to bear. The final life story was one of drug addiction.

I understood that Juliana's purpose was to come to our realm and have a full and meaningful life. She was to share love and friendship as well as push herself and all of us beyond our limitations. She was always going to exit but wanted to leave the planet with the biggest impact, inspiring all of those who knew her and loved her to live amazing powerful lives. We were always going to feel tremendous sadness and grief around her life, which in turn would open us up to loving more.

In the dream, I saw and felt the sadness and heartbreak the final life would have caused and realized she had chosen to leave in the best way she could. Quick and easy, like pulling off a band aid. Here one minute, gone the next.

When the movie ended, the dream shifted; we were now both sparkling and laughing. We sat down at a table with the rest of our family; they were all sparkling as well. There was a giant map on the table. We each plotted a course to take, intersecting paths along the way.

I woke wondering if we have all chosen our paths before arriving on this planet? Do we know our exit points?

Cross-country

I'm back in Pagosa; I jumped in my car and drove straight to New Orleans. I left early the next morning and drove 17 hours to Santa Fe, New Mexico, and stayed in a little hotel for the night. I arrived in Pagosa the following morning.

It's crazy that no matter how I break it up, it still is 33 hours in the car. I actually like driving. I feel like being stuck in a car with nothing but open road is a great opportunity to talk to God. Now, I talk to Juliana. In the final minutes of my drive on the second day when I was sleepy and seeing blurry-eyed, I felt like my daughter was sitting next to me. She was keeping me awake and focused. If I squinted and looked with an offset view, I could see a form in the seat. It was a swirling translucent rainbow pearl essence and very much present in the car. I like to believe it was Juliana.

My stay in Pagosa Springs was brief. I needed to be there for Malaya's graduation as well as Alyssa's wedding and a divorce court date, then I was free to go. I had decided to give Utah a try, knowing I could continue my flight training with Utah Helicopters.

Alyssa's wedding

A beautiful day in the mountains, a gorgeous bride and lots of tears. Alyssa is Juliana's best friend. All of the people showing up for this wedding knew this would be a challenging and glorious day for the lovely bride. We all wanted to show up and bring as much love and support to this sweet girl on her special day.

The wedding was picture perfect, so touching and profound. I could feel Juliana everywhere. I could see in the teary eyes of all the guests that they knew she was here to witness the ceremony of her beloved best friend. The day had a certain charge to it and my skin responded with goose bumps. At one point, I talked to two adorable children who knew Juliana personally (she had been their babysitter). I knelt down to their eye level and asked directly if they could see Juliana; they both said yes. Children are amazing!

Journal Entry 6/17/18

My dreams are fascinating and vivid, full of faces I don't recognize and exciting places that seem vaguely familiar. When I wake and they fade, I wonder if this is what dying is like: waking from a fantastic consuming dream only to have all of it disappear off in the distance.

I've been in Pagosa for almost two weeks and am feeling unsettled, antsy. I have been studying nonstop for my written FAA exam and am happy for the intense focus.

The bigger picture here is I am still very much grieving. I am still feeling uncertain and wobbly about my divorce. I still am unsure about my life and the course I need to take, probably because I do not know what I actually want to do with the rest of my life. I'm looking for clues in every person and circumstance. I'm continuing working on my flying, and I know it's at least something I can do for the time being that is constructive and challenging and fun. The time is going to pass regardless, so I may as well work on something that can give me a future.

A message from Juju

Hey, Mama!

Yes, baby.

You can do this, I love you and you have always been strong and amazing; you need to see it.

Love yourself, let go, and be confident. Create all you desire in life. YOU GOT THIS. You have to go through this fire, this pressure; it's the only way you can come out the other side as a diamond.

Chapter 8
July

Utah, the Next Journey

I decided I needed to continue moving forward. Being in Pagosa still didn't feel right. My adorable small town felt stagnant, suffocating, and depressing.

I chose to try out Utah for a bit.

I have dear friends in Utah who offered to let me stay with them for a while. They are my chosen family and love my children as their own. They were very connected to Juliana as well and I felt like spending time with them would be good for all of us in our healing process.

I am welcomed with loving, warm arms. I'm given a safe place to rest and gather my broken pieces. This family shares love and laughter and acceptance and they are open to talking about Juliana.

I notice that the more we talk about her, the better I feel.

Glory, my friend, is a sweet, kind, open-hearted lady. She is a dream interpreter and a psychic medium in training. She had been training to develop her gifts for quite some time and being in her presence felt nourishing to my soul.

We would spend our mornings sipping coffee and talking about our dreams and intentions for our lives.

She too was grieving the loss of Juliana, and together, we opened ourselves to communicating with her.

One thing I noticed is almost every morning, as we would chat, birds would fly into her window, crashing into the glass as if they were trying to join us. One of the times, I stepped out and picked up one of the stunned creatures and held it in my hands for a solid ten minutes while it got its bearings then flew off. Life in her home felt powerful and magically synchronistic.

Glory invited me to join her in a medium ship class she was taking. I happily accepted.

The ladies in the class were amazing. They were all powerfully connected to spirit and would bring in disembodied loved ones who wanted to share with the group. Juliana came through with messages of love.

The woman who ran the class invited me to tune in and bring someone through, explaining that we all can do it if we want to. Connecting to spirit is normal and natural, we just need to quiet down our minds and feel from our hearts.

I successfully tuned into a father figure who wanted to share love with his daughter, who was present in the room. The feeling for me was so subtle and delicate. It was like trying to harness a breeze with my open hand, or pulling a feather through mud without dirtying the bristles.

Journal Entry 7/4/18

In Utah, I arrived yesterday at Dave and Glory's house. I immediately felt a sense of peace and comfort wash over me as I entered their home. This family is wonderful and being around them feels nourishing.

Glory and I talked about Juliana non-stop, crying about how much we love her and laughing about all the funny things that happened in the brief life of this darling girl.

I shared a story with Glory about how there were many times I wondered if I did a good enough job as her mother. I wondered if she knew how much I loved her.

I brought back one specific torturous memory of her eyes.

Juliana had vision problems as a young girl, and we had her checked out by an optometrist who prescribed glasses. She wore the glasses for maybe a year then stopped wearing them. I never brought her back to the doctor. She never complained about her eyesight, and I just let it go. Her eyes never crossed my mind until later when she was in college and she had found her old eyeglasses and started wearing them again. (They were maybe 10 years Old.) She said that she had a hard time seeing all through middle school and high school and was happy to be able to finally see. When she told me this, my heart sank, knowing that I had completely failed as a mom. I never took her back to the eye doctor. How could I let something as important as her eyesight slip past my priorities?

I cried to my dear friend about how deeply I felt regret for not taking care of my daughter as I should have.

I wish that I could take this back, that I could have a redo and be a better mother.

I guess this is bound to happen—memories of the things I did wrong, the feelings of regret, the things I could never change or fix were bound to wash up on the shore of my memory.

Journal Entry 7/6/18

I woke with a beautiful dream lingering in my thoughts. Juliana is music.

Yesterday, Glory and I were talking about how much Juliana loved music and how she was actually tone deaf for most of her young life. Sometimes, when she would practice, I would cringe and want her to stop in fear that she would be made fun of, but something inside me could not discourage my daughter. Instead, I would encourage her to keep practicing.

Sure enough, with years of singing lessons and perseverance, Juliana was able to both sing and create her own music. She taught herself to play the guitar and was able to leave us with some beautiful songs in her wake.

The dream I had was a vision of this exquisite girl who had an absolute determination to express through her body musically. Her body was challenging for her and would not cooperate but she continued to train it and make it sing. Her vocal cords had to be whipped into submission by her soul that so desperately wanted to serenade us all.

The feeling I got from the dream was that she is no longer inhibited by her body but is now her true angelic expressive self. She is the music that wanted to come through.

Journal Entry 7/13/18

Paddle boarding

I brought my paddleboard with me to Utah and already paddled out on a pristine lake a few days ago. I was on the water at 6 am wanting to experience the sunrise. I was all-alone in the foggy, cool morning dressed in sweats. The water was glassy and I had a sense of gliding on the sky as it was reflecting into the crystal lake.

Today, I chose to paddle on the Great Salt Lake. It is a huge, smelly body of water. The lake's saline content is so high, the only creatures that can live in the water are brine shrimp. The entire lake is loaded with sea monkeys. I walked out past the shore and brine flies jumped on my board. With my music playing in my ear buds, I paddled away. I made it out about a mile and a half then had a very clear realization that I could invite my spirit daughter to join me. Sure enough, she was there right alongside me. I could feel her presence and enjoyment as we moved along the surface of the water. I started singing out loud, as I knew this is what she would have done.

Chapter 9
August

Journal Entry 8/8/18

I flew today. It was a gorgeous, clear day in Salt Lake City, Utah. I had another lovely message from Juliana.

As I was arranging my flight bag in the helicopter, I put my hand in to one of the pockets and pulled out a dangly diamond earring, (not a real one of course, but it still serves as a symbol from my beautiful daughter). The crazy thing is, I had been using this bag for the past several months and filling the pockets with things like my cell phone and keys. I hadn't noticed the earring before.

I love receiving these sweet reminders that she is here. Thank you, sweet daughter.

Memory~ in the spring of 2016, the year Juliana graduated, She walked in to the house and announced to the family that she wanted either a raccoon, a skunk or a fox. We all looked at her strangely. I reminded her that all three of those animals were illegal to have as pets. She shrugged off my words and went about being an 18-year-old. Two days later, sure enough, I got a call from a friend who had cut down a tree; they were

chipping up the branches when they heard the screams of a baby raccoon. My friends asked if I knew of anyone who would be willing to raise the baby as it would need lots of care at its young age. I called Juliana.

Every four hours on the dot, Juliana would bottle feed the baby.

Luna was a healthy, happy, little rascal of a raccoon and Juliana was her mama.

Two weeks later, Juliana found a baby skunk. She adopted Stella into her little fur family and cared for the two as if they were her own biological children. She was attentive and thorough; she learned about everything these two needed to grow into healthy happy animals. (She would have been a fantastic mother.)

In the summer, she packed up Luna and drove the now teenage rambunctious raccoon to Florida she wanted to give Luna to a woman who could rehabilitate her and introduce her to her rightful life as a wild animal. Juliana packed up her car and drove solo across country with her raccoon, sneaking Luna into hotels along the way. Luna was her pride and joy and knowing that she may never see her baby again was admirable, especially for an 18-year-old girl. She was wise beyond her years.

Stella, a much calmer, easier animal, became a sweet house pet that didn't make a peep. She was a funny creature who

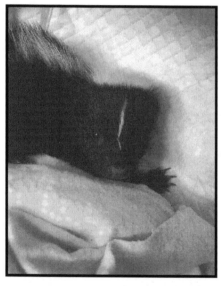

ran around the house stomping and skidding at any sign of danger. Stella lived with Juliana when she went to school. She created a skunk haven under her bed and a ramp for Stella to climb up at night; the two would sleep together most nights.

Stella was in the car accident with Juliana and survived. I'm happy to say that Stella is now with a loving woman who has the right licenses to keep her. She is loved completely.

Chapter 10
September

Journal Entry 9/18/18

Today, I woke with gusto. My mind felt clear, my body woke early and I have a feeling of wanting to share with the world. My daughter came through again very clearly yesterday. I went with my friend Glory to a medium practice gathering. This group of ladies practice communicating to spirit a couple times a month and have allowed me to join them while I am in Utah. I am almost finished with my stay here and I feel like this is most likely my last session with them. One of the wild things about this group is they are all very friendly with each other but do not share their stories of their dead. They let these stories emerge in their practice sessions.

It feels like a game of putting puzzle pieces together as they pull through info, direct it to one of the group and piece by piece assemble a picture of a loved one with a message. I love being able to witness this. I love the feeling in the room of swirling spirits just wanting to communicate and lovely humans working on opening up and connecting with these spirits.

Juliana came through.

At first, the woman who brought her through said, "I have a young lady here; she feels like a daughter." Then she honed in on me and said, "She's here with you." I absolutely knew I would be hearing from Juju. I gratefully listened and confirmed the things this woman was saying.

She saw a picture of me sitting on a counter in the kitchen and having deep conversations with my daughter. The woman said Juliana was wanting to thank me for these times and to let me know that she felt loved and supported by me and cherished those conversations. She also wanted to tell me that she admires me and my fearless approach to life. Juliana wanted to acknowledge the fact that her life had many challenges, especially when she was a young teenager, and even though she was distant from me, she could feel my love and support and encouragement. She said she knew I loved her. She also said she is with me now and loves me.

Ahh, my sweet daughter, thank you for making my world brighter and for giving me these wonderful morsels of info. I love hearing from you and with each bit of communication, I feel more and more settled and assured. I know you are here. I know we can continue to develop our relationship. I know you came here to teach me how to open my heart and to love with all of it.

I'm feeling so much better, honey, knowing you're here and safe and still very much a part of our lives. I'm going to continue practicing and opening myself to even clearer communication. I want to be able to see you for myself.

Blog Post 9/20/18

Something shifted the day before the 18th; I woke with an amazing feeling of clarity. My eyes shot right open as I felt the heavy mental fog lift off my tormented brain. This feeling was so intense that it was all I could talk about for the past two days. I feel wonderful!

It's been nine months since my daughter left this world. I have been writing every day, spilling my heart out to my journals trying to make sense of my world.

Every single day, she would bombard my thoughts.

Every single day, I would have intense emotion flooding my cells.

Every day, tears would flow, so much sometimes that I couldn't be in public.

Every day, I questioned my course of action and my purpose on this planet.

When am I going to feel better?

How long does it take to grieve the loss of a loved one?

When will I actually let go of the sadness?

When can I just be happy to be alive?

This whole process has been one of learning to let go of needing to control anything, especially my emotions.

Learning to get up, even if I don't feel like it, to get moving in a general direction, and to realize it's ok to not feel ok.

I had to give myself permission to slow down and feel my way through the murky waters, as they were not clearing anytime soon. Then miraculously, after almost 9 months to the day, I just felt good.

As a mother who has experienced the gestation period of making a tiny baby inside my body, I am wondering if death too has a gestation period.

I'm not saying by any means that this is the time limit for grief. I'm just happily reporting a shift in my emotional state. I am absolutely welcoming this shift and feeling so excited to move forward in a positive and optimistic way.

Maybe what I am actually experiencing is the birth of my own transformation.

Thank you to all of you who have been my web of support and love. Your caring and kindness have been the strands holding the broken pieces together.

I made it through the tunnel and can stand upside down with a huge smile on my face.

Journal Entry 9/25/18

I am in Idaho at my mother's house. I have a few days to spend with her as I'm not on the schedule to fly till the end of the week. I arrived yesterday and was able to help my mom harvest fruit from her many loaded trees. We cut, cleaned and preserved fruit for most of the day.

Her house is quiet and comfy. She lives a pretty simple life alone. I treasure spending time with her, listening to all her stories.

My mom's house is full of ghosts. She talks to them out loud (maybe this is where I get it). I can feel the presence of two of my grandmas and Juliana.

Hi, ladies, I love that I can feel you here.

Hi, Juju.

Hi, Mama.

Oh goodness, why do tears fall when I think of you?

To help you see better.

I don't have much to say but I am happy to feel your presence and love. It seems this is all that needs to come through, proof of existence and love.

I talked with my mom about creating a symbol for us when one of us dies. We agreed on a black pony. We both love horses.

When I was young, I had a gorgeous black pony named Licorice. I wonder what happens to our pets when they pass on? I wonder if Juliana knows Licorice?

Being in Utah was very good for me. Sharing daily with my dear friend Glory has been extremely healing and enlightening. I was amazed at her dedication to developing her deep connection to spirit. She is a part of a dreaming community and presented at a conference a few months after Juliana's death. With her permission, I have included her beautiful words, interpreting a dream Juliana had two days before she died.

"Juliana's Dream" Understanding Pre-death Dreams © Glory Nelson, B.Msc

We often have "warning dreams," or dreams of someone who we later find out has passed away. We also hear about pre-death dreams of those who are terminally ill. Hospice workers and death doulas have shared their experiences of what their patients say, see and hear before they pass. But what about a lovely dream from someone who is about to leave the physical world and doesn't know it yet? Was this a sign, an indicator of what was to come? Join me as I explore the dream of a 19-year-old who tragically left this realm two days after she had it.

The News:

Just a few months ago, I received the horrible news that my best friend's daughter—whom I treated like my own—passed away in a tragic car accident. My heart was shattered. While on the phone with my friend, she said, "Juliana had a dream about you and me two days ago and we were going to call you today, so you could help us figure out what it meant." I couldn't really ask about the dream in that moment because of the shocking news, but when we arrived at her life celebration a few days later, I had to ask.

I was given permission by Juliana's mother to share her dream for this presentation.

Juliana's Dream, This Is How She Re-told Her Dream to Her Mother.

I am on a stage. The auditorium is full of people. I am nervous. I am either singing or playing the guitar or both. You and Glory are backstage. I look over at you guys and you reassure me. I start singing, and I really get into it and close my eyes. When I open my eyes, everyone is gone. I look back at you guys, and ask, "What should I do?" You both say, "Keep going, it's okay," and so I keep singing. End of dream.

The spiritualist community believes the soul knows when it will leave the body. Did Juliana's soul know?

Juliana's Death

Juliana was driving home for the holidays. She was driving from Denver to Pagosa Springs, CO. This is roughly a 5 to 6-hour drive. It was the middle of the day when she tragically drove off a cliff, just 28 miles away from her home.

Sitting with the Dream

When I look at Juliana's dream, I notice that the audience is gone. When we received the police report, they ruled the accident as her falling asleep at the wheel. She was ejected from her vehicle but was completely intact and no blood was found at the scene, which means she died instantly. In her dream, she spoke about closing her eyes, which for me feels like a good indicator that she did fall asleep. Many people were concerned that she had committed suicide, but this dream has given family and friends a sweet reminder that Juliana was in a good and healthy place. She was excelling in school and in life. She also had her pet skunk in the vehicle with her and it survived the crash; we knew she would never put her animals in danger. In my understanding of her dream, the backstage represents a curtain between us, acting as the veil. Our encouragement feels very significant. We told her everything was going to be okay, that she would be okay.

> The potential to experience a powerful pre-death dream is built into human nature...from a limitless variety of people—women and men, the young and the old, the powerful and the weak.
>
> K. Bulkeley and P. Bulkley

Communication

The night I found out about Juliana's passing, I had a dream. **Dream:** *I am in Colorado with her mother and we are going to stop by and visit Juliana. As we arrive at the door to her apartment, she walks out and looks happy and whole. She tells us she is late for work. She gives us both a hug and walks away. I am so happy she is still alive. Why did I think she was dead?* End of dream.

Upon waking, the gut-wrenching realization hits me: she is gone. On a high note, she had come to visit me in my dream and she looked great. Since then, I have had several dreams with her. In one dream, she is pushing me to share her dream at this conference.

Waking Synchronicity and Signs

We went to Colorado for her life's celebration, and it was very healing for all of us, especially for my daughter who has been Juliana's best friend since they were a year old. On Christmas Eve, we drove home. On the drive, we tried playing my iPod several times, but it never played, so we listened to the radio. Two days later, I drove my car for the first time since the trip, and the iPod started working. It played, "Because" by the Beatles. This was one of Juliana's favorite songs. I remember Ju and my daughter trying to harmonize and sing it when they were ten-year-olds. I couldn't believe it; was this a sign? After I told her mom what happened, she informed me that Juliana had been practicing that song to perform at a show she was doing in March.

I can't help but believe our loved ones give us signs from the other side to let us know they are okay, and to comfort us. Juliana leaves glitter and diamonds for her mother and siblings to find. When we talk about her, the lights flicker. She sends me hearts and unicorn-shaped clouds. I think she knows that if anyone would pay attention to her tricks, it would be her mom and me. Maybe that's why we were in her dream.

In reading *Dreaming Beyond Death: A Guide to Pre-Death Dreams and Visions* by Kelly Bulkeley and Patricia Bulkley, I can say that in most cases, pre-death dreams are a preparation for the transition. These dreams not only help the person who is transitioning come to terms with their death, but they allow those he/she leaves behind to feel some sort of comfort and closure. In researching for this paper, I was unable to find literature regarding pre-death dreams from healthy young people.

Conclusion

As a dreaming community, we are all aware of the importance of sharing our dreams. Our sixteenth President, Abraham Lincoln, was a dreamer who loved journaling and sharing his dreams. "Members of Lincoln's cabinet recalled that, on the morning of his assassination, the president told them he'd dreamed of sailing across an unknown body of water at great speed. He also apparently revealed that he'd had the same dream repeatedly on previous occasions ..."

We may find it impossible to know when we will have a pre-death dream; therefore, it is important to continue to share our dreams with those we love. We never know when it will be our last. It may be the beautiful goodbye we leave to the world.

I am so grateful Juliana shared her dream with her mother that day, for so many reasons. I truly believe that Juliana's dream is a gift of comfort to her family and friends. She left us with an image of what she loved to do!

This paper was very difficult for me to write but it was very healing. Thank you for letting me share with you Juliana's Dream.

Chapter 11

October

Journal Entry 10/4/18

I am home in my little rental in Colorado. I still oscillate back and forth. I suspect this is just going to be my new norm; my emotions have a way of sneaking up on me.

Today, I had a breakdown after finding a pair of headphones I had given to Juliana a couple years ago. I know she listened to these headphones continuously, and holding them in my hands made me miss her. I could feel the giant hole in my heart once again. After a few minutes of crying on the floor, I remembered I could talk to her, so I wrote her a letter.

Dear Juliana,

I miss you so much. Even though I love so many things about this life, I still get overwhelmed at the amount of pain that is present, and many days I think that living is too much.

My mind likes to take over and worry. I worry about how I'm going to make it through this life. I worry about your siblings. I want to be there for them and help them with their pain and yet I'm just barely able to handle my own.

I worry that I'm going insane and that talking to you is just my imagination. I want so desperately to believe you are here and I can communicate with you.

I also selfishly want you to be here in the physical with me. I want to hold you and love you and be your mom.

Do you have any advice?

Life is for living, loving, creating and playing. All of it is a game. Just play the game. Get really good at it. Make beautiful things. Share as much love as possible. Give of yourself. Think about others. Be bold. Be brilliant. You got this!

I'll see you sooner than you know, we will all be laughing together and happy, really happy. It's who we are, it's who you are. Happy is natural.

How can I be happy?

Time heals all wounds. It just takes time; be patient. Really awesome things are coming. You're going to amaze yourself.

Thank you, I love you!

I love you too, Mama, so much. I always have and always will. Get some rest; tomorrow is a new day and it's going to be great.

Journal Entry 10/12/18

As I was falling asleep last night, I quietly asked for any

last notes I needed to add to this book. Was there anything I was missing? Any other little tidbits of information that would make a difference in other people's lives? I was woken at three in the morning deep in dreams. In my dreams I noticed that a part of me was witnessing the dreams. An observer self was taking notes wanting to remember the dreams, even though the stories were nonsense. I wondered if this was my true self—a subtle force that watches all of my life as it unfolds. Then I wondered where this part of me resides. Does it live in my physical self or is it in the ether realm, the beyond? Is this part of me with my spirit daughter?

I imagined it's like playing a game of virtual reality and I have chosen to wear the headset and blind myself from everything outside of myself so I can be immersed in the game. I wondered if we are all so immersed that when our game is done, we will take off the headset and see all our loved ones sitting right there next to us.

I had a very clear understanding that the reason I have been able to communicate with spirit daughter as I have is simply because I believe it's possible. Our beliefs create our reality.

I was also aware that it's not a special talent that only a few of us have, but in fact, we all can communicate if we just open ourselves up to it.

Communication comes in many forms and paying attention is key.

I understand that our loved ones are doing everything they can to let us know they are fine and they are still with us. They want us to know this so we can continue with our lives in a glorious way.

I was also reminded of a special message I had received right after Juliana died. A young lady told me my daughter was doing her best talk to us. This girl was a part of our community but not real close to any of the family. She was reluctant to contact me, but Juliana was in her mind very clearly and needed her to share a message of love and well-being with us.

I took her message to heart and the things she talked about have come to pass. She told me I would be connecting to Juliana but needed practice.

Feelings

I am in Texas. I have been here for a few days. I have chosen to come here for a change of scenery and to visit with a man I adore. I have found so much comfort in the arms of others and know this whole process has made me vulnerable enough to actually allow myself to be loved.

The one common thing about all the traveling is my feelings come with me everywhere I go. I cannot escape them. I am an overflowing well of emotions these days.

Navigating with a purely emotional body has been quite a challenge. I am unpredictable and explosive one moment then weepy and laughing the next. I feel supreme joy and heartache in the same breath, then I feel exhausted from feeling and my eyes shut heavily not wanting to open.

I feel like the palette of my life's painting has many new colors that I am not familiar with. I just keep smearing on whatever I can, but the colors are all mixing and leaving a mess. Maybe I just need to stop painting for a bit and stand back to have a solid evaluation. In all this, I do have a tremendous sensation of gratitude underlying my feelings, and I thank God this exists or the rest of it would be unbearable.

Journal Entry 10/25/18

Juliana was in my dream. She killed a daunting attacker with an axe by chopping forcefully it into his neck and then chest. I was with her and amazed at the power and strength she had.

Chapter 12
November

Perspective

It's really challenging to look at a life from only one perspective. All of life is multifaceted, rich and beaming in many directions.

To capture even a tiny bit of a person's essence is a huge task.

I reached out to some of Juliana's friends, knowing that if I am having a hard time processing, I'm sure they are too. I asked them to share some of their best stories and memories of Juliana to include in this book.

A Message from Alyssa

Juliana and I became friend in the seventh grade we were inseparable and had the most amazing bond, I thought of her as my sister. We knew so much about each other's lives and secrets. We supported each other through our challenging young years and knew that no matter how far away the other was we would always be close.

She was my ray of sunshine. She was my date to all our high school dances and events; she was always by my side.

Any time I had a problem with my family she would offer to let me stay with her. I believe I slept in her bed for almost a year.

We laughed so hard over some of the dumbest things. From watching the dogs play to swinging on the pole in the dance studio, or floating down the river and hitting our asses on all the rocks. I loved listening to her sing in Town Park. I loved all the heart to heart conversations, the many hours we would spend chain smoking and talking and crying in the snow.

One of my favorite memories of Juliana is when we were at Town Park and she dropped and broke her pipe. She super glued her hand and flip flop to the pipe trying to repair it.

I also loved when she would pretend like she was a T-rex.

Last November we got in an argument over her maid of honor dress for my upcoming wedding. This argument lasted until the day I lost her. It was so dumb; I wish I could take it back. I honestly would have gotten married in jeans if it meant that I could have my Juju back.

I have suffered through loss many times in my life but this one was the absolute worse.

Since her death, there hasn't been a single moment that she hasn't been on my mind or in my heart.

She still walked with me in the wedding, in my heart and on the memorial pictures I had framed. Now she hangs all through out my house. My daughter still calls her daily, and tells me she misses her.

My daughter also tells me "anti Juju loves you".

I feel her everywhere. Even though not in the physical I know she's here, looking over us, protecting us and singing to us all.

Treasure every moment of everyday with your loved ones for tomorrow is promised to no one.

My only wish is to hold Juliana one last time and tell her how sorry I am and how much I love her.

A Message from Bri

Juliana and I have been friends since the eighth grade. We have so many memories together, too many to count.

She was not only my best friend; she was my sister.

We did everything together. We had been living together for a couple years before she passed. We would get up every morning and make coffee. Sometimes, I would have to make her a cup and bring it to her in bed just for her to get up!

We had our differences but no matter what, we always loved each other. Our relationship was something nobody could ever take away from us. We shared something no one else would understand.

I miss sitting with her while she would get ready and listening to her get so mad because that her eyeliner wasn't even, or her hair didn't look good. She would always come to me to fix it.

I would tell her how beautiful she was, and make her smile when she wanted to cry.

I miss being in the car with her when she would sing along to the radio and dance like a crazy woman.

She always knew how to make someone smile. All she had to do was be a dork.

One time she and I were riding on a four-wheeler (under the influence of course); we ending up rolling the four-wheeler. She hit a tree and I was stuck under the four-wheeler. She pulled me from underneath it and just held me. She went with me to the emergency room. She walked around the halls with blue rubber gloves on her feet just to make me laugh.

She will forever hold a place in my heart, along with every memory.

I talk to her a lot as if she's right next to me. I leave her messages too; it makes me feel better for a little while.

A Message from Frankie

Juliana and I were roommates and were really good at butting heads; mostly, it was because of our competing relationship with Bri. When it was just the two of us, we would get along and shared some amazing memories.

About a week before the accident, Juliana and I got into a serious argument over my snake and her fish (stupid right). Something she and I had in common was we both had to be right 99.9% of the time. We had a bit to drink and that argument was so bad, it took a few days to make amends. I hadn't planned on talking to her about it because I didn't know how to approach the subject, but before she left, we shared a cup of coffee and an American spirit (light blue) and talked it out. I think about this every day. I have so much regret because there were definitely things left unsaid.

Juliana would always look out for others before herself, which is something I admired in her.

I remember her running to the store before you visited just to grab some honey. She knew you liked honey in your coffee.

Juliana was very good at making impulse decisions. One night, she decided she wanted fish (mind you, it was 8pm).

She got up and asked me to go to the store. She picked out a half dozen fish and a tank. She put a few things in the tank and changed the price tag. I looked at her and said, "You are going to get us in trouble." She said, "Shut up, you didn't see a thing."

Juliana gave us the idea of putting up baby gates in the apartment so the dogs wouldn't go into the rooms. One night, she and Bri were fighting; she was trying to ignore us and tripped hard over the gate, nearly eating drywall and she said, "Is the gate ok?" (She broke it.)

The night before the accident, she face-timed Bri and me. She was finishing packing a few things. She asked if I wanted her to leave the light on for the snake; while she asked, the snake was running through her hair. She was so weird sometimes.

I am thankful to have shared so many memories with her in the short time I knew her. She was wonderful.

A Message from Michell

The first time I met Juliana was in our Americana class. She was so fun and bright and I was shy and quiet. I was involved in some boy drama and she helped me through it. I spent the night at your house; she gave me a dress to wear for a date I was planning with the boy. I never used the dress; it was too pretty to use for a stupid boy.

A Message from Caitlin

I originally met Juliana in massage school. One of the first memories was in class, we were assigned to watch each other and analyze our partner's stride then to mimic our partner's walk. Juliana was my first partner; she made sure to over-exaggerate my stride pattern, hips forward, spine leaned back and my head forward. She looked like she was doing the limbo. Juliana described my walk as a gangster. I busted out laughing so hard, so did the rest of the class.

As time went on, Juliana became one of my closest friends. We shared a lot and supported each other through good and bad times. At the time, my father was going through cancer.

There were days where I just couldn't talk about it, but Juliana could read my face. She would take a moment to let the tears out and we would give each other heart to heart hugs then go jam out to music. On one of my rough days, we ended up talking and hanging out listening to music and supporting each other emotionally and spiritually. We sang "The Sound of Silence." She showed me a video she made with her guitar and her amazing voice; it gave me goose bumps. We sat in her car for so long, it ran out of gas in the parking lot.

Juliana changed my life!

A Message from a Friend I Shall Not Mention

One of my favorite memories was when we went to your house to take pictures with guns and we broke one of Darren's mounts. We all freaked out and tried to glue it back together with eyelash glue. To this day, no one knows about this but you.

A Message from Maria

So many memories and moments with Ju; here are some of my favorites.

We were at the house and it was a huge bonfire. I'll never forget all of us were drunk and having a blast. I walked up to her and said, "Ooooo, a piece of candy," then licked whatever was on her hand. Little did I know, it was acid. She was dying of laughter because she just witnessed the beginning of a long trip.

We used to sing "Somewhere over the Rainbow" together and I'd be so jealous of how confident she was. I hated my voice.

We would drive around in the old Chevy, and of course, we'd get high as kites. We almost went in a ditch a few times, but man, did we have fun singing our hearts out. We'd joke about how we were gonna get married one day so I could be a part of the family, but I always was. That was the best part!

When we were in theater together, we'd always mess around back stage. I'd honk her boobies and she'd go with it, grab them and jiggle them around. She loved her body so much, and that's what made her so special! She never let anyone tell her different!

My last but favorite memory. When I came home from basic training, I was driving around town just reminiscing. I saw her and Alyssa at the park. I pulled up and she was so confused. It took her a minute before she realized it was me, then that smile lit up and it was amazing. She ran up to me with no shoes, and gave me the biggest hug. I jumped on her and I never wanted to let go! That was also one of the last times I saw her. That hug and that moment were truly amazing! So much love from her!

After she died, the night before Christmas, I was crying outside trying to talk to her. I was asking where she was and how was she doing. I hoped she was happy. I told her I would always love her.

That night, I told my family that I called a certain spot on the couch, and no one could sit there. Everyone gave in.

The next morning as I sat down on that spot, I noticed a small seashell on the armrest. I looked blankly and asked everyone in the house if they knew who put it there, or if someone had lost a seashell. No one had put it there or remembered a shell being on the couch. No one in that house had been to the beach. I started crying because I knew it was Ju; she left me a sign telling me that she was listening. I believe she is somewhere on a beach. I keep that little shell; it has brought me happiness knowing that she is still around.

A Message from Mel

I remember Juliana and Brie dancing and singing in the bedroom. When Brieanna stayed with your family, I would call crying, wanting my daughter to come home. Juliana would calm me down, assuring me my daughter was okay. Sometimes, I felt like she was the adult.

I will cherish my last memory with Juliana; we had coffee and a slice of Oreo cheesecake at Starbucks. It was so simple, but I knew she loved it.

Juliana will always be a ray of sunshine. When I think of her, I can't help but smile. She is missed so much. I loved her as my own.

A Message from Casey

We were at our cast party from the burlesque show. I was feeling sad that night and not really wanting to be social. When I pulled up to the party, Juliana was out side. She and I sat and talked for a while she played and sang one of her favorite songs for me, (I believe it was a stairway to heaven.)

She was so beautiful and peaceful and lovely while she sang. I will never forget her.

That girl was a force of nature with a heart as big as a building and a temper to go along with it. She was a delight and an inspiration.

Now in her wake, everything in life has a different texture. Maybe this is her gift to all of us to leave in such a way that our world will be forever changed—more expansive, less trifling.

Dear darling Juliana,

I miss you deeply and love you so much. I am forever grateful to have known you and am happy and excited to continue to know you. I look forward to the day we can see each other again. I live now with the sweet tinge in my heart reminding me to pay attention and enjoy the moments, no matter their content. All of life has a strange new appearance, and I want to do my best to not waste a single second. I am embracing all these new sensations of twisted emotion, knowing that in the long run, they are paving a way to a greater, more expanded vision of life.

Blog Post 11/18/18: Spirit Support

Eleven months today, our beautiful Juliana left this world. It's been a whirlwind of an experience.

I haven't been posting in my blog as my attention was intensely focused on studying and passing my flight exam and check ride.

I'm happy to announce the instrument rating is now behind me as I passed with flying colors, literally.

The magnitude of the preparation has been all consuming. I didn't know that I actually had the ability to study with such dedication. The flying practice itself was extremely challenging and many days I wanted to give up.

During the check ride, (after we had been already flying for over an hour,) I was feeling extreme doubt and exhaustion. My examiner was doing his best to cause a disorienting situation by changing my instruments. He placed sticky notes on three of the critical instruments then expected me to find my way with only use of a oscillating compass, all the time remaining on course.

I was privately in a panic doing my best to figure out where I was and continuing to fly with precision.

My body tightened up as I felt unbearable uncertainty creep in.

I then had a sweet sensation, the feeling of a gentle hand on my shoulder and a warm assuring whisper in my ear. Juliana was with me, she said, *"Mom you got this, calm down, breathe, just relax you can do it, it's just a game".*

The rest of the flight was smooth, easy, relaxing I knew I had my angel daughter with me.

I am so incredibly grateful to know that death is not the end. Our moments in life are here to teach us about our own strengths and abilities. We get this precious time to play the game of life, and to embrace each other in all of it.

I have recorded as much of the past tormenting year in my journals and will be sharing them with all of you in a book titled SUNN. I hope that in sharing these personal moments I might inspire you to love more deeply, cherish the time you have and open up to the loving support that is available from spirit.

With so much love~S

Author's Note

I am sharing this book with you in hopes that you too will be able to find some peace and perspective in the wake of loss.

Loving is a part of living, and losing someone doesn't mean the love stops.

I think in this process, the most challenging thing to understand is love never dies. Love is the delightful connecting force that binds us all. We must open to the many forms of love that are available. It is so tempting to close down and shut ourselves off in fear of the pain that comes with loss. The pain is actually the doorway to a greater expanded love.

I am happy to report that the worst of the storm has passed. I believe being open to communicating to my daughter has helped.

I will continue to open even more, to quiet my mind, to look for symbols and signs that my daughter is sharing her love.

As this book comes to an end, the true journey is only beginning. I am going to continue developing my connection to the world beyond and continue living the biggest and brightest life I can possibly create. I know it's all temporary, and I hope to make it absolutely amazing.

I will continue to accomplish the bucket list my beautiful daughter left for me and to add a few things of my own.

Thank you so much for reading my words; you now are a part of this story.

Made in the
USA
Columbia, SC